BEYOND *Life*

Insights on Living, Growing and Dying

SIRSHREE

YogiImpressions®

YogiImpressions®

BEYOND LIFE
Published in India in 2011 by
Yogi Impressions Books Pvt. Ltd.
1711, Centre 1, World Trade Centre,
Cuffe Parade, Mumbai 400 005, India.
Website: www.yogiimpressions.com

First Edition: October 2011

Copyright © 2011 by Tej Gyan Global Foundation

Cover design by Shiv Sharma

ISBN 978-81-88479-82-5

Printed at: Repro India Ltd., Mumbai

Contents

You Cannot Die

Why does death occur? Why is the fear of death put into the minds of people? Is death the one and only final truth? Is there life after death? You may have these and many more questions in your mind. You will find answers to all these questions in the conversations appearing in this book, presented through an imaginary storyline in a very simple manner and language.

This book is based on a series of conversations between various seekers and Sirshree, as well as on discourses imparted by Sirshree on the subject of death and life after death.

While reading the book, please keep in mind that the simplicity of the language does not undermine its message. The language is kept simple so that each and every one can understand the message clearly.

It is dangerous to have half-baked knowledge on this very important topic of death and life after death. For this reason, whenever Sirshree delivers discourses on this subject, it is announced that whoever wants to leave can do so right in the beginning as no one should leave midway into the discourse. Hence, it is of utmost importance that you read the book completely. Do not draw conclusions after reading only a part of the book. Please read it with an open mind and without any prejudice or preconceived notions. Read it from beginning to end and make a fresh beginning in your life – a life where you understand that you cannot die – a life known as Supreme Life.

Sirshree says, "If knowledge about death and life after death makes your present life beautiful, and if understanding it brings about a positive change in your life, then you have understood the message correctly." He adds that the knowledge imparted in this book is not just for clearing doubts and gathering information, it is also for changing your life completely by bringing about a total transformation.

Though the book is in a conversational format, Sirshree does not use the word 'I' to refer to himself in the entire book. As a Self-realised master who expounds and espouses only about the existential experience of consciousness, Sirshree does not use the word 'I' the way most of us do in conversation, be it the ones captured in this book or otherwise. This is because Self-realisation is the very transcending of the 'individual I' and being stabilised in the 'Universal I'. For the direct experience of the 'Universal I' and for opening the doorway for such stabilisation, you too are invited to attend the Magic of Awakening (MA) Retreat designed by Sirshree.

Thank you,
Krishna Iyer
Editor

The Urgency

"I have everything, yet it seems like I have nothing," Sameer said to himself, no longer sure if what he we was going through was spiritual inertia or just plain lethargy. "But, in a few minutes, I am sure it will all be clear." He smiled at this thought as he managed to squeeze his six-foot tall body into his car. His mobile phone flashed a reminder – Clarity appointment – Ashram – fifteen minutes.

"I remember," he told his phone as he hurried to get his car out of the parkway of his lavish apartment.

Sameer, thirty years of age, was the Chief Executive Officer at Marigold Software. He owned a house at one of the poshest places in town. He had everything money could buy, but he still felt like he had nothing. He was the CEO but still felt like a clerk. He was well travelled and socially well connected but felt that all he had done was visit many airports and make many acquaintances.

Despite his material success, Sameer managed to keep his feet firmly on the ground. He gave a lot of credit to his spiritual master for where he was today. This is what Sameer wrote about himself on his blog:

I am Sameer. People call me Sam. I am a human being first and a seeker and disciple next. A CEO and writer last.

Educated as a lawyer, I hold international certifications in business law and taxation. My best education, however, is what I have received and continue to receive from my spiritual mentor, Sirshree Tejparkhi.

I run a niche mobile applications development company. I volunteer every weekend at Tej Gyan Foundation, an organisation founded by Sirshree, dedicated to creating a highly evolved society. I love writing and translating and have authored as well as translated a few books in the field of spirituality and self development. Plus, I have published various articles and papers in the field of software law.

So, what was wrong with Sameer? Externally, nothing. Internally, everything. In the three years that he had been with Sirshree, he had gained immensely. Yet he was at a point where he felt empty within. Despite having achieved so much, he still had this feeling that he was going nowhere. He wrote about this feeling to Sirshree and requested an appointment. That was where he was heading now.

What attracted Sameer to Sirshree was the simplicity, clarity and logic with which he taught about the direct experience of the Self. Sameer, a voracious reader, had come across one of Sirshree's books. In them, there was one question that had resonated with him:

Seeker: My question is 'Who am I?'

Sirshree: You are nothing with the potential of everything. Hinduism talks about the sense of everythingness. Buddhism talks about nothingness. Both are the same and this is what you shall experience in the Magic of Awakening Retreat.

Having read this, Sameer attended the retreat. His spiritual journey began at that retreat, where he experientially realised his innate nature of feeling nothing and having everything. Sameer, who was once so focused on making money, realised that spirituality is everything. Sirshree had taught him to continue doing what he was doing, but be grounded in spirituality and be centred on the experience of God. He was asked to practise spirituality in the stock exchange, meditation in the marketplace and tranquillity in the theatre. He liked the practicality of his teachings and continued to attend the follow up sessions. On one such occasion, when he had an opportunity to attend a question-and-answer session with Sirshree, he asked a question that had been troubling him for a while.

Sam: Why is it that even after experientially knowing the Self, the mind is so strong? Why is it that I feel that the ego is so strong?

Sirshree: What you experienced in the retreat is an experience of self-realisation – what Zen masters call satori. But the mind comes back and claims the experience as one that it experienced. It does not realise that only when it [the mind] is not there, the Self can experience Itself. Continue to listen and understand. The journey has begun. It has begun with self-realisation.

The journey is from self-realisation to self-stabilisation. On stabilisation, the contrast mind does not arise again. [The contrast mind, which signifies that mind which compares and judges everything, splits everything into two – white or black; good or bad. It is this mind that gives rise to fear, worry, envy, insecurity, deceit, anger, etc. In fact, it is the root cause of all the miseries in human life. It is only present in humans. It is the one which blocks us from seeing the truth.] Self-realisation could be a one time experience. In self-stabilisation the Self is stabilised in Itself.

Sirshree would like you to practise this meditation for the next few days, which shall help you in this journey. Count the number of times you use the word 'I'. Whenever you say 'I', give it a number. With awareness, you shall become aware of the use of the word 'I' before you say it. Then try to avoid saying it. Use the passive voice as an alternative. Instead of saying "I did this," say "this happened."

Sam: Is that why Sirshree never says 'I' while referring to himself?

Sirshree: It does not matter how you use the word 'I' after self-stabilisation. And you have to practise this meditation only for a few days till you become clear about the difference between the real 'I' and the illusory 'I'.

Sam: I shall practise this, Sirshree. No, this shall be practised.

This meditation had helped Sameer recognise many facets of his ego. But of late, he felt a spiritual lethargy and wanted to shake it off. Hence, the meeting with Sirshree.

Sameer reached the Ashram and walked into the room where Sirshree was seated. The room was small and clean with white walls, and a window lined with peach curtains. There were cushions placed on the floor for the disciples to sit on. Sirshree sat on a chair from where he spoke his enlightening words peppered with laughter. Sameer had secretly thought of writing a book on him titled 'The happiest man in the world'.

SIRSHREE: Sameer!

Sam: It is wonderful to see you again.

SIRSHREE: Yes! What brings you here today? Is it the vacuum you referred to in the letter?

Sam: Yes, Sirshree. I have grown spiritually. I live a balanced life. I do understand that there is nothing else in the universe – but God, Self or Consciousness. Thanks to you, I understand that the body is only a medium for the Self to experience Itself. Yet I feel a vacuum within. I don't see an urgency to spend enough time on the application of your teachings. My business takes precedence. I am obsessed with my business goals. You have asked us to spend at least eleven minutes in silence practising the art of *samadhi* [one of the final stages of meditation] every day. I can't bring myself to do it. I love your teachings. I contemplate on whatever you say. My life is transformed. But yet my life does not reflect the fact that spiritual growth is important to me. What should I do?

SIRSHREE: There is nothing to do. There is only the need to understand.

Sam: That's the beauty of your teachings! You always ask us to focus on first things first. I forget that I operate from the standpoint of 'doing' and continue to raise questions based on it. You are in the domain of 'being' and lead me back there.

SIRSHREE: Yes. Let me now ask you a question: If you were to die today, will Sirshree be happy or sad?

Sam: (*bewildered*) Well, I have seen you unshaken in so many situations. I don't think you will be either unhappy or happy. You are beyond these. A stabilised master does not become happy or unhappy. And I can't see how this pertains to my original question.

5

SIRSHREE: You will see. For now, just assume that Sirshree does get happy or unhappy. So what do you think? Will Sirshree be happy or unhappy if you die at this very moment?

Sam: Hmmm. Sirshree, I think you will be unhappy.

SIRSHREE: Why?

Sam: Because I am one of the key contributors to this foundation; I also help in translating your teachings into English. I am like a brand ambassador. If I die, who will carry on the torch to make Tej Gyan Foundation global? It would be a loss to the foundation. That will make you unhappy.

SIRSHREE: (*chuckles*) Sirshree shall surely be unhappy if you die, but not for this reason. Sirshree shall be unhappy because if you die now, you shall create hell wherever you go.

Sam: (*shocked*) I don't understand! In your teachings, you have said that there is nothing like heaven and hell and it is all here and all in the mind. And now, you say that I shall create hell. Do you mean to say that I shall go to hell if I die today and that shall make you unhappy?

SIRSHREE: Before we resume with this line of questions, tell me why are you so agitated?

Sam: Because you are indicating that there is something *after* life. I always thought that there is nothing beyond this life. And I love the scientific approach that you bring into everything. You did not just

preach that there is only all-pervading Consciousness. You took us by the hand and showed that
Consciousness is experiencing Itself through the
body. But, now this thing about 'after death' and
that I shall create hell! I am confused and maybe
agitated due to that.

SIRSHREE: Are you willing to listen to the illogical?

Sam: You have explained that there are seven legs of
the mind – the seven negative habits of the mind
on which it survives. And you have explained that
the fifth leg is that of logic. Before you expounded
what self-realisation is during the retreat, I did
give up logic. I had to give it up. Else, the Self
could not have been experienced. Whatever you
have taught so far has transformed my life. I think
I am willing to listen to the illogical.

SIRSHREE: Maybe you have given up logic *logically*. The
logical framework of the human mind imposes
limitations – a major hurdle to be overcome so
that the subtlest can be known. The mind has to
understand that there are things that are not in
its realm. It has to be at least open to listen to
what it finds illogical and try it out. But this is
akin to listening to the illogical *logically*. However,
as the seeker progresses, faith increases automatically – faith in the Guru or God or Grace. Then
he becomes open to the illogical that life presents
in his way. Then he becomes open to listening to
the illogical without any qualms.

Sam: I find this fascinating. I also know that you have said that this happens automatically. All one has to do is to continue listening and be in *satsang* [a spiritual discourse or sacred congregation]. That is another beautiful part of your teaching. I am here today because I have been listening to you in satsang. And that has caused my transformation. I know that as a part of what is happening, I may progress to develop more faith. Whatever I have listened from you and read in your books so far has helped me immensely. Hence, I am surely willing to listen to the illogical and try out what you say.

SIRSHREE: You have to be pushed more to give up logic. But right now it's okay. It is at the end of the spiritual journey – towards the state of self-stabilisation – that logic is the biggest hindrance. There, the doubting mind doubts the very experience of the Self. It checks and interferes. This checker has to be shown the door. But at this stage, do not give up logic. But listen with an open mind.

Sam: Yes, Sirshree. Absolutely.

SIRSHREE: So, you were asking whether Sirshree meant that you will go to hell.

Sam: Yes. And probably that will make you unhappy. But I don't believe there is something like heaven or hell.

SIRSHREE: Sirshree said that if you die today, you shall create hell wherever you go.

Sam: But will I go somewhere? I thought death is a great blackout. Nothing more; nothing beyond. You are born. You die. Finished. It is all over. I have heard you say that there is no reincarnation. And that actually helped me understand and accept you as a master because you were one of the few spiritual masters to denounce reincarnation. And now you say that I shall go somewhere. Where?

SIRSHREE: Reincarnation, the way people believe it to be, does not exist. But that's a topic for another day. The fact is that the journey continues after death. There is a Part Two to this Part One of life. Continuing onto Part Two does not mean returning to Part One. This understanding of Part Two will bring about the urgency in spiritual growth that you seek. Also, Sameer – Sirshree would like you to read something before the next meeting.

Sam: (*Sensing that Sirshree is indicating that the meeting is coming to an end.*) Before the meeting ends today, I wanted to convey that I still did not understand what you meant when you said that you will be unhappy if I die and that I shall create hell wherever I go. Is that a *koan* for me? [*Koans are stories or verses that defy the logic of the human mind and provide insights into Truth that transcends duality*].

SIRSHREE: It is a koan of sorts, but something that shall be cleared when you meet Sirshree again. For now, read the story of Nachiketa before the next meeting exactly one week from now.

Sam: I have read the story in the *Amar Chitra Katha* comics during my childhood. I remember the story vaguely. I shall revisit it and surely meet you next Wednesday. I leave, seeking your blessings.

SIRSHREE: Thank you for the opportunity of serving you.

A Story about Death

Sameer left the Ashram with Sirshree's last words ringing in his ears. Sirshree always ended his discourses with those words.

"What a wonderful message," Sameer thought. "Someone of Sirshree's stature saying this shows how humble and reverential he is. But then, now he is talking about something beyond the conceivable world!"

Sameer drove towards his office. On the way he got stuck at a traffic jam. Sameer was swearing and fuming all the way. 'Gifts of the twenty-first century – cars, mobile phones, laptops – are all there to save us time, but they are taking up more time than ever before and nothing is left for any soul searching,' he thought. He decided to stop at a book store on the way to pick up a book on Nachiketa.

It was 3 pm by the time he got a parking spot and walked into the book store. As he entered, a blast of cold air greeted him. He had been there many times before and he knew every section. Instrumental music played in the background. It was a cosy place. Sameer went straight to the religion section to search for the book he wanted. He spent a few minutes, but found nothing. Disappointed, he left and picked up some lunch at a nearby drive-through restaurant as he drove to his office.

Sameer was a workaholic. He couldn't get himself to practise what Sirshree referred as 'doing nothing successfully'. He had a few meetings lined up. After finishing them, he glanced at his watch. It was 7 pm already. He stretched himself out like a cat, breathed out, and got a cup of hot coffee. He was tired but had some energy left to do some research on Nachiketa on the Internet. He was amused by what he read. He was ready for his next meeting with Sirshree.

SIRSHREE: Sameer!

Sam: Yes, Sirshree. It's wonderful to be at your feet again. You told me last time to read on Nachiketa. I did. It is an ancient story. I brought a printout.

SIRSHREE: Good. Can you read the story?

Sam: Maharishi Aruni performed a *yagna* [a religious sacrificial ceremony] called the *Vishwajeet* yagna. In this yagna, all your belongings are donated – your house, wealth, land and cattle. After a few years, Maharishi Aruni's son Uddalak Rishi also followed in his father's footsteps. He too gave away all his cattle and wealth in a sacrificial ritual. Uddalak Rishi had a very bright son called Nachiketa.

SIRSHREE: Good. I see that you have done your homework. The real purpose of sacrifices in the olden days was not just to give away your house, wealth or cattle. The real, all-important purpose was to give away the ego. Uddalak Rishi did not understand this. The purpose of all rituals points only to the Self. Tell me

12

what else you read about Nachiketa – the bright, young and mature boy. Nowadays, you call such children as child prodigies. Yes, continue the story.

Sam: During the sacrifice, Nachiketa observed that most of the cows that his father was donating were old and frail. They could hardly eat or drink, nor could they yield any milk. They would end up being a burden for whosoever received them. Nachiketa felt that this could be regarded as a sin on his father's part, which in turn may prove to be detrimental for him in the other world.

He went to his father and cautioned him about the feeble cows. But his father was so busy with people around him that he did not pay any attention to what his son was trying to tell him. Seeing no other way, Nachiketa thought that he would ask his father to donate him as well, since he was also his father's wealth, and he could also serve the person who received him. This, he thought, would help mitigate some wrongdoings on the part of his father.

He began asking his father repeatedly as to whom he was being donated to. His father got angry on his persistent questioning and said, "I give you away to Death; I donate you to Yamaraj – the Lord of Death." These words came out in a fit of rage, but Nachiketa took them as his father's command and set out for the abode of Yamaraj.

Sɪʀsʜʀᴇᴇ: Many-a-time parents do not really understand their children and unknowingly utter some wrong words which leave a deep impression on the child's mind.

Sam: That is an interesting insight on anger.

Sᴉʀsʜʀᴇᴇ: Those who wrote these tales and intertwined them in the Upanishads [ancient Indian scriptures] and other texts were very intelligent. They embedded messages right from parenting to right living so that people heard them and got inspired. Alas, most people listen to them only as stories. Anyway, Sameer, continue the story. Now comes the most important part.

Sam: On the way to Yamaraj's abode, Nachiketa began to contemplate. 'There are three kinds of sons and disciples – the first kind are those who can anticipate what their father or guru wants and carry it out without an explicit order; the second are the kind who complete a task as soon as they are asked to; and the third are the ones who do not do anything even when they are asked to.

These three kinds fall into the highest, medium, and lowest disciplinary categories. Even if I do not fall in the first category, I am definitely in the second, because I have always done what my father asked me to. Then why has he sent me to the Lord of Death? Surely, there must be some task that he wants me to complete'.

Thinking about this, he reached the abode of Yamaraj. The Lord of Death was not present at his abode. Nachiketa waited for him for three days without eating or drinking.

A Story about Death

SIRSHREE: Consider the irony that is brought out at this juncture. When a person tries to run away from death, death constantly hovers around him; whereas when he himself seeks death [*personified as Yamaraj in this story*], it eludes him. Yes, continue.

Sam: Nachiketa had fearlessly approached the door of the Lord of Death, but he was not there. Yamaraj returned after three days and was surprised to see a child waiting for him. He offered Nachiketa food and water and enquired about his visit. Impressed by the child's determination to meet him, Yamaraj said, "You waited for me without food or water. I offer you three boons. You can ask me for anything you wish."

The first boon Nachiketa asked for was that his father should no longer be angry with him and should start loving him once again when he returned home. In addition, he should never be a cause of worry to his father; thereby, his father should be able to sleep soundly and happily every day of his life. Yamaraj granted Nachiketa his first wish. Thus, the first boon was for his father's well being.

Nachiketa asked for the welfare of all people as his second boon. He said, "I have heard of a place where there is eternal happiness, where there are no miseries, where there is no hunger or thirst, where a person never becomes old or dies – it is known as 'heaven'. As my second wish, I would like to know the procedure for performing the yagna to attain such a place." Yamaraj readily gave him all the details for performing the yagna. Sirshree, the third boon that Nachiketa asked for is something I don't quite understand. Shall I read it from the printout I have brought?

SIRSHREE: The third boon is what Sirshree wants to speak about. Go ahead and read it.

Sam: Nachiketa told Yamaraj, "Some learned men say that everything is over when a man dies, just like plants and animals perish and dissolve into the earth, so that nothing is left of them. Whereas others say that it is only the body that dies, the soul within is immortal. When the soul departs, the body dies. Depending on its deeds, the soul goes either to heaven or to hell. It then undergoes rebirth based on its deeds and receives the fruit of its deeds of previous births and performs new deeds. It is caught in the cycle of birth and death until it attains the Supreme Self." Nachiketa then posed his third query. "I would like to know which of the above is true and understand it in all its depth."

SIRSHREE: Many versions of the story omit what he meant by 'in all its depth'. It means that he didn't want to know it just in words, but understand it at an experiential level. This is because only that knowledge which can be experienced is true knowledge. True knowledge alone can help man take right decisions and lead a life of unconditional love.

Continuing with the story, Yamaraj was taken aback at Nachiketa's third request. He realised that he had underestimated the child. He reflected that few people asked such questions.

Sameer, this is an important point. Everyone uses the mirror, but few are those who look into the mirror and think, "Am I this body? If I am not this body, then who am I?" Likewise, few people are inquisitive enough to know about death. Most are terrified of death and do not want to hear anything about it or even be reminded of it.

What else did you read? What more does your printout say?

Sam: Yamaraj tried to gauge the seriousness of his intentions in asking this question and also tried to distract him by offering him any other wish he desired.

He told him he could absolutely get all the power, riches and luxuries of the world. He also tried to explain to him that it was a very profound question and even great, learned men and deities had been unable to understand this secret, even after it was revealed to them. Being a very difficult subject to understand and explain, it was better if he asked for some other boon. Nachiketa, however, was determined to know the answer to this particular question. He said, "I cannot ask for any other boon. And where will I find a better person than you who knows all about death? Please give me the answer to my question."

This reply was music to Yamaraj's ears, who was only testing the young child. He was impressed by the steadfastness shown by Nachiketa.

He began, "The element that is the Soul or Consciousness is present in every plant, animal and human. This soul is a part of the Supreme Self and is manifested through the body. The Supreme Self, which is unmanifested [*unexpressed in any form; the Formless; the Nothingness with the potential of everything*], was present before everything, is present and pervades everything, and will continue to be after everything. The unmanifest is even beyond Brahma.

"Brahma, Vishnu and Mahesh [Creation, Perpetuation and Destruction, personified] have been regarded as the Trinity responsible for this world. The unmanifest or Supreme Self is the origin of these three. The Supreme Self has not been created by anybody or anything, because it is the essential origin or the ultimate source. Once man knows the soul, he loses the fear of death.

"With time, the body disintegrates, but not the soul. It lives on. It has lived on. Consciousness existed even before the body, before the world was created. The unmanifest precedes manifestation. Manifestation is an illusion created by the unmanifest to know itself. When the manifested got associated with the body due to the illusion created by the unmanifest, an individual was born. The ego [*the feeling of apparent separateness from*

everything else or the feeling of being a separate entity]
within the individual induces the fear of death.
When the ego of the individual is destroyed by
knowledge, only then will true self expression
without any fear occur."

Yamaraj continued, "Man reaps fruits according
to his deeds. He either progresses in his journey
or descends to lower levels and remains stuck in
the cycle of joys and sorrows. There are two ways
you can live your life – one is the selfish way and
the other, the selfless way. If you are engrossed in
accumulating more than what you and your family need without caring for others, you are being
selfish. If you perform good deeds, work for the
welfare of others, never hurt anybody, always obey
and serve your guru, constantly seek knowledge,
worship God, imbibe positive qualities, get rid
of negative ones, and always seek the company
of learned and noble men, you are treading the
path of selflessness. This is how you are fulfilling
all your worldly duties as well as preparing well
for the welfare of your soul by imbibing good
qualities and performing good deeds."

In this way, Death [Yamaraj] unfolded its mys-
teries. With this understanding, Nachiketa could
experience the unmanifest within him and attain
self-realisation. He had understood the purpose
of life. Totally satisfied, he returned to his father
– knowledgeable, fearless, and free from all defile-
ments and evils of the body and mind. He became

SIRSHREE: Good, Sameer. Now tell me what you understood from the story.

Sam: I liked the part about Nachiketa's patience and his desire to understand the truth about self-realisation and about death. The self-realisation part of the story could be grasped easily. You have enabled us to experience the difference between the manifest and the unmanifest in your retreats. I understood that part.

But this thing on death was too much. What is the meaning of the sentence '…the soul lives on'? What I found funny about the various versions of the story is that everywhere it is said, 'In this way, Yamraj explained death to Nachiketa'. But which 'way' is not described anywhere.

SIRSHREE: (*chuckles*) True. But the story still has some significance. The key points to be gleaned from the story are:

* This story is an indication to understand the game of life and death and thereby lead a life of love and joy.
* Death is a teacher that is tough from the outside but gentle and beautiful from within. Death is the best teacher to learn about death.
* Children are pure and innocent; they are far removed from cunningness and deceptions of

adult life. Hence, they are much better equipped to look Death in the eye and question it.

* Many-a-time, parents do not really understand their child and unknowingly utter some wrong words that tend to leave a deep impression on the child's mind.

* Everyone uses a mirror, but few look into it and think, "Am I this body? If I am not this body, then who am I?" Likewise, few people are inquisitive to know more about death.

* The ego inside the individual induces the fear of death. Complete knowledge about death makes man fearless.

* While living in this world, we are preparing ourselves for the journey ahead. There is life after death, and once you know this, you won't waste even a moment of your life in trivial pursuits. Every incident will become an opportunity to develop your patience.

Sam: All true, except for the last point. What is all this about 'life after death'?

Sɪʀsʜʀᴇᴇ: It is simple. You practise energy healing. So what do you know about the energy body?

Sam: The fact that it exists. Everybody has an aura around them and that is the energy body.

Sɪʀsʜʀᴇᴇ: Every human being has four sheaths. These, however, seem to be a single entity. Let us suppose that a person is wearing first a vest, then a shirt, followed by a sweater, and finally a coat. These can be likened to the four sheaths.

But, to an observer, the vest, shirt, sweater and coat do not appear to be distinct. In fact, from the outside, it is just the coat that can be seen. The person who has worn the four garments is separate from these garments. However, since the clothes cover him, he cannot be seen. This person depicts the true Self which gets shrouded by the four sheaths.

In this example, the person wears one layer over the other. However, in case of the human body, the four sheaths are intertwined. The four sheaths from periphery to centre – for the sake of understanding – are:

* the *physical* sheath – it is the fourth or the outermost sheath, which can be compared to the coat;

* the *pranic* sheath – it is the third sheath, which can be compared to the sweater;

* the *mental* sheath – it is the second sheath, which can be compared to the shirt; and

* the *causal* sheath – it is the first or the innermost sheath, which can be compared to the vest.

The physical and the pranic sheath have been referred to as the gross body. The mental sheath and the causal sheath are the subtle body.

When a person dies, only the two outer layers, termed as the gross body, are shed off. Referring

to the above example, when someone dies it is
like the coat and the sweater are removed. The
shirt, the vest and the person wearing them are
still alive; they are not dead. The coat is akin to
our physical sheath, which can be seen from the
outside. It experiences aches, pains and other difficulties. We do our best to do away with these.
However, we do not experience these pains in
deep sleep. There is no physical pain even after
what we call 'death'. This implies that whatever
happens during deep sleep is something similar
to death.

What we understand as death is the death of
the two external sheaths. It is similar to someone
taking off his coat and sweater. The coat is the
physical sheath or the external layer. The sweater
is the second sheath, the pranic sheath, which is
composed of the *prana* or vital energy or breath.
When you pass an electric current through a wire,
a magnetic field is created all around it. If there
is a pair of spectacles through which you can
see magnetic fields, you will be able to see that.
Similarly, due to the presence of prana, a magnetic
field exists around the human body which is called
the 'aura' of that person. The aura is seen to be
consisting of certain colours. When the prana or
vital energy departs, the aura also disappears.

Aura is present around every person, though
it cannot be seen with the naked eye. It can,
however, be seen with special instruments. Today,

scientists have invented such devices. With their aid, you are able to see the aura around people. The effect of the aura present around a person is what is called 'personality'. Those who have a strong personality have a strong aura around them. The aura shrinks in people who are usually fearful and timid. It disappears completely after the death of the gross body.

Sam: Wait a minute, Sirshree. You are great when you are in a flow. But for us mortals, it is impossible to grasp all of this so speedily.

SIRSHREE: Let Sirshree repeat this in other words. What we know as 'death' is the death of just the two external sheaths. The two inner sheaths and the real Self which is immortal are still alive.

Let us take up yet another analogy to understand this very important aspect. Imagine that you are seated on a scooter, to which the body of a car has been attached. Even the handle of the scooter is similar to the steering wheel of a car. You are riding a scooter, but from the outside it appears as though you are driving a car. Here 'you' is symbolic of the true Self. The scooter represents the two inner sheaths or the subtle body. The body of the car symbolises the two external sheaths or the gross body.

When a person dies, it is as if the car body has been removed. You are driving only a scooter now, therefore, you feel much more comfortable. You are no longer bothered about parking space. You can scoot through traffic much faster. The problem with the car was that it required a lot of space and it was difficult to manoeuvre. It has now become much easier. You were driving a scooter even when the car body was attached, although it seemed as if you were driving the car. You are driving the scooter even after the car body is detached. Then where is the question of death? What difference has it made? This is the incredible phenomenon you have to understand. This is the enigma you have to fathom. This knowledge will teach you the art of death.

That's all for today, Sameer. Contemplate on this and come back. Thank you for the opportunity of serving you.

The Journey of the Subtle Body

The next week, on Wednesday morning, Sameer was busy drawing. Every once in a while he threw a ball of paper into the trash can. Sameer called it 'Trashketball'. His trash can was brimming as he had missed only a few shots.

As he sat on his desk staring at the blank paper, he realised that it was difficult to start writing or drawing anything unless there was some inspiration. Although he was bad at drawing, he could pull off geometric shapes. He was trying to draw symbols representing the analogies of death as Sirshree had mentioned. Sameer's talents lay in his ability to categorise, package and relate Sirshree's teachings to the world and its problems. Sketching was clearly not his forte and this was one of his initial attempts. Finally, after nearly two hours of struggle, he managed to sketch the two analogies. Proud of his little triumph, he filed them in his bag.

He was quite excited by the time he reached the Ashram at noon. Although there were some doubts gnawing away at his mind, yet he decided to focus on understanding what Sirshree was saying and then ask about his doubts.

SIRSHREE: So, Sameer, what have you contemplated on?

Sam: To help me understand better, I've drawn some pictures of both the shirt and the scooter analogy. Can you tell me if these are correct?

SIRSHREE: These are well-drawn and correct representations of the analogies. However, make just one small change. In the second picture, where you have drawn and explained the scooter-car analogy and written 'after life', you can change it to 'Part Two'.

Sam: Why 'Part Two'?

SIRSHREE: The term 'Part Two' has been coined to signify a deeper meaning. When a new term is introduced, the mind stops for a moment. It does not tend to ignore it as a normal word. Part Two is completely and totally different from Part One – the life here on Earth. It is much longer than Part One too. Hence, Sirshree prefers calling it as Part Two.

Sam: You have always had a way with words. I still remember the word 'knowlerience' you coined to signify a combination of knowledge and experience. Why you prefer calling it Part Two is clear now. But I have still not grasped the whole thing. I have read on the Internet that there are five bodies – *annamayi* (physical/food sheath), *mannamayi* (mental sheath), *pranamayi* (vital/energy sheath), *vigyanmayi* (intellectual/knowledge sheath) and *anandmayi* (blissful sheath). And you say there are four. Then you also talk about the gross and subtle body. So, are there two bodies as in gross and subtle? Or four bodies? And what about the fifth – anandmayi – the blissful body?

SIRSHREE: There are five sheaths. It is better to call them as four sheaths belonging to the fifth. These four sheaths constitute two bodies belonging to the fifth. The purpose is to reach the fifth.

Sam: I did not understand.

SIRSHREE: There are four overlapping sheaths and the fifth is the one wearing those sheaths.

The outer two sheaths – the physical and pranic sheaths – make up the gross body and the inner two – the mental and causal sheaths – make up the subtle body. In the coat analogy as discussed last week, the fifth one wears the clothes. That is the Self – the real You. In the car analogy, you are the entity who is driving the scooter. But don't call it five sheaths. It is better to call it as four sheaths of that entity. Do not call it three bodies. It is better to call it two bodies of that entity.

Sam: What entity?

SIRSHREE: The Self. The Consciousness. The Supreme. The purpose of life is to reach the fifth. Let us understand this with the help of a small story.

There were five drunkards. They held a party. Drinks were flowing freely. When they were left with the last bottle of wine, they elected to keep the bottle aside for the next day. They also decided to divide the contents of the bottle into five equal shares. Having made up their minds to drink it the next day, they went off to sleep.

Four of them woke up in the morning and found that the bottle was empty. They then saw the fifth person lying in an inebriated condition. They shook him awake and asked, "Did you empty the bottle? Did you drink the entire wine?" He replied, "I had only my share." The four looked at him incredulously and screamed, "But you have emptied the entire bottle!" He explained, "My share was at the bottom of the bottle. To reach there, I had to go through your four shares. Only then could I reach my share. And it was very gratifying indeed!"

What the fifth person said is noteworthy. Going through the four sheaths, we have to reach the 'fifth' – the Experience of the Self, which is very gratifying. To reach the 'fifth' is the goal of spirituality.

It is the source of all-encompassing bliss. The aim of those who tread the path of truth, wisdom and God is to reach the fifth – the true Self. This is the meaning of spirituality. People have their own notions of what spirituality is supposed to be. They believe that spirituality is something that you get into after the age of fifty and that you have to sing devotional songs, chant, and perform all kinds of religious rituals. The real meaning of spirituality is to reach the fifth, the real Self, which is covered by the four sheaths. It is not that in order to reach the fifth, you have to shed the four sheaths. The purpose of life is to access the fifth while being encapsulated in the four sheaths or two bodies.

Sam: If the ultimate goal of life is to reach that 'fifth', then what is death?

SIRSHREE: You have understood so far that death is the shedding of the two external sheaths which is like the removal of the car body, or taking off of the coat and sweater. The two inner sheaths – the mental sheath and the causal sheath and the one governing them are still alive. The rider is still riding the scooter. The scooter still exists. When this will be clear to us, we will understand that what we have known as death all our lives is not actually death. It is merely the death of the gross body. The journey still goes on; it does not stop after this incident. It continues in the form of the subtle body.

When a child reaches adolescence, do you say that the child has died? You don't, because you know this adolescent is the same person who was a child until some time back, and has now just grown up. And then when the adolescent grows up to be a young man, do you say that the adolescent has died? You do not say so. Likewise, when the young man becomes old, do you say the young man has died? No. But when the old man becomes a subtle body, you say that he has died. In fact, it cannot even be said that he has 'become' a subtle body because the subtle body was already present. It is only that the two outer layers have fallen off. Out of ignorance, people start crying at the so-called death of their near and dear ones.

What would have happened if you had complete knowledge? If you were able to see the subtle body after the death of your loved ones, would you be as unhappy? Of course not. Supposing you were able to see the deceased person around you in the form of his subtle body – sitting, standing, sleeping – the only difference being that he is not able to talk to you. If it were so, you would not feel as sorrowful since he continues to stay in your home as before. If the subtle body of your grandfather or other relative stays with you for many years, you would not have any fear or grief associated with death. Then one day, that subtle body too would depart. Would you become sad then? You won't because, as it is, you could not speak to him, he was almost not there – he could only be seen. This does not actually happen. It has just been stated as an example.

After the dissolution of the gross body [*the physical sheath and the pranic sheath*], you believe that the person has died. But in reality, he is not dead. His journey goes on. This can be understood with one more example. What happens when you go to see your friend or relative off at the railway station? He boards the train and after some time the train begins to pull away. You can see him until the train leaves the platform. You wave out to him as long as you can see him. You stop waving once he is out of your view. Sameer, do you then think that the person has died because you are not able to see him?

Sam: No, I don't. I cannot see him but I know that he is continuing his journey. The only thing is that I don't have the power to see him any longer.

SIRSHREE: Thus, understand through this example that a person does not die when you stop seeing him. His journey continues.

The vision and listening capacity of man is limited. A dog has a stronger sense of smell. An owl can see more clearly in the dark. An eagle can locate its prey on the ground from high up in the sky. Similarly, there are other creatures that have highly developed senses as compared to humans. Humans cannot see the subtle body whose physical form has been shed. They think that the person has died. And then comes the crying and the mourning. There is no end to what ignorance can make you do!

Sam: This means that what we call death should be actually called 'so-called death'!

SIRSHREE: Yes, 'so-called death' is a much better term. It can also be called as the transition from Part One to Part Two. Sirshree prefers calling the journey beyond not as life after death, but as Part Two.

Sam: So, what happens once the subtle body is donned? What happens after so-called death?

SIRSHREE: Sameer, in fact there are four questions – what happens long before so-called death, what happens just before so-called death, what happens just after so-called death, and what happens long after so-called death.

Sam: One couldn't have put it better! It's a wonderful way to expound the questions.

SIRSHREE: *(smiles)* The answers are more important. Therefore, contemplate on these four questions and in the next meeting give me your answers, at least for the first three. Thank you for the opportunity of serving you.

The Four Key Questions about Death

Sameer felt a sense of completion, similar to how he always felt after every meeting with Sirshree. It was like finding the missing pieces of the puzzle of death. It was surprising how a feeling of having heard something beyond the mind can bring peace of mind. As he drove he noticed the crowd – drivers, cart pullers, hawkers, cops, businessmen. He never really focused on them, but today he viewed them with a different understanding. They all appeared as robots to him. Each of them was engrossed in the illusion of their material wants and desires and many of them were still stuck at the bottom of the pyramid. Do they have any time to think about life and its purpose? Nobody likes their existence to be questioned, he wondered.

He remembered some lines from a poem by William Wordsworth:

> *'What is this life if, full of care,*
> *We have no time to stand and stare?*
> *No time to stand beneath the boughs,*
> *And stare as long as sheep or cows.'*

He realised that everyone understands death as being the ultimate destination. No one has been able to escape it. Even those who want to go to heaven don't want to die and go there. But he had now begun to understand the mystery of death. A sense of gratitude filled him as he parked his car.

The week passed by. Over the week, he was so engrossed in his work that he forgot about contemplating upon the four questions given by Sirshree. He remembered on the day of the appointment and felt ashamed. He looked at the pictures he had drawn, thought about Sirshree's questions for some minutes, and convinced himself that he was ready to meet Sirshree.

SIRSHREE: Sameer, let us begin today by summarising what you have understood so far.

Sam: I have understood that we have four sheaths, which we carry with us all the time. And there is the fifth which wears these four sheaths. He is like the driver of the scooter. This fifth is the real 'I', the true Self. The key point I have understood is that in so-called death, the two outer sheaths are shed.

SIRSHREE: The remaining two sheaths subsequently undergo a long journey. A lot more has to happen with these two sheaths.

Sam: Yes. I am keen to know what happens afterwards.

SIRSHREE: That is the third and fourth key question about death. But let us come to the first key question. What do you think happens long before so-called death?

Sam: We live. We wake up; we eat; we work; we sleep.

SIRSHREE: The interesting part is the sleep part. When a person drifts into deep sleep, the subtle body could wander out of the gross body, travel to different places and return.

What happens when sometimes you suddenly wake someone up from deep sleep? The subtle body has gone out travelling and returns in a flash at that very moment. Some people experience a headache after this. This happens because the two bodies merge all of a sudden, due to which their alignment does not occur as smoothly, leading to discomfort.

If we could see the subtle body, we would observe that it is very similar to our gross or physical body. It is attached to the gross body through the navel; that means the two bodies are joined together. There is a flexible string called the 'silver cord' attached at the navel that binds the two bodies. The subtle body travels to a lot of places and comes back. A lot of times these travels are manifested as our dreams. On visiting a new place, sometimes some people feel a sense of déjà-vu – a feeling they have already been there before, in spite of being there for the first time.

How does that happen? There must be an explanation. It suggests that the subtle body wanders out of the physical body, travels around and then returns. The experiences during those outings get recorded in your sub-conscious mind.

Death is nothing but severance of the silver cord between the gross body and the subtle body. Who sleeps when you go into deep slumber? Have you ever asked yourself the question: 'Who sleeps?' When you are lying down to sleep, thoughts are going on in your mind. After some time, the thoughts stop appearing and you drift into deep sleep. Have you ever noticed the last thought you had before you drifted into deep sleep? You will never be able to pinpoint that last thought you had. In the morning, you start having thoughts again and you experience yourself to be awakened. So, Sameer, who is it who sleeps?

Sam: Who sleeps? Well, I sleep.

Sirshree: Sameer, you never sleep. The 'real you' never sleeps. Actually, who had slept and who is awake? Only thoughts had slept, and now the thoughts are awake. The Consciousness that is the screen on which all thoughts arise is always awake. It has never ever slept. You say 'I slept and I woke up'. In reality, it is your thoughts that slept and woke up. The 'knower' never slept.

You go through profound experiences of life and death in your sleep every day. The feeling of the body is lost in deep sleep. You have been experiencing death every night before your so-called death. You have been seeing a lot of places through your dreams. During samadhi, you can experience the 'fifth', that is the Self Witness, the driver behind your four sheaths. Through meditation, man arranges for his death while alive. He experiences death in his conscious state.

Sam: This thought is beautiful. Meditation is arranging for a death-like experience while being alive. I have experienced this thoughtless state many times through the meditations you have taught me.

SIRSHREE: The Self experiences Itself in a thoughtless state. The Self shines when the mind drops. That is akin to death while in the conscious state. Deep sleep is when Consciousness is not aware of Itself.

Sam: Thus, long before so-called death, man experiences death-like experiences. He experiences thoughtless states and he experiences the subtle body being separate from the gross body, especially in sleep.

SIRSHREE: Yes, in a thoughtless state, the 'fifth' experiences itself. And in the state of sleep, sometimes, the subtle body travels outside the gross body. Now what do you think is the answer to the second question – what happens just before so-called death?

Sam: I have understood that the two outer sheaths are shed off on death.

SIRSHREE: But that is on death. And the remaining two sheaths subsequently undergo a long journey. But understand what happens just before death.

The silver cord connecting the physical body and the subtle body is cut just before death. You must have seen or heard that a lot of people who are in pain or suffering, suddenly become calm just before death and a smile appears on their faces.

Why would that happen? This is because just before death, people begin to understand a lot of things. They begin to realise that what they were considering death, and fearing and crying over, is not death. All at once, they develop an acceptance of all those things.

A lot of insane individuals seem to be completely cured moments before their death. It is astonishing for people witnessing it. They are completely sane and peaceful, moments before they die. This means that their insanity will not continue after the death of their physical body.

The same has been witnessed in people suffering from physical illnesses and pains, which implies that the sufferings of the physical body do not continue in the subtle body. People realise something just before their death which fills them with peace. This does not necessarily happen with everyone. It depends on the understanding gained by the person during his entire life, as well as by Grace.

In some instances, towards the end, people recall the same thoughts during death that they have harboured throughout their lives. They think 'What will happen of this matter now? What about my family? What about my relatives? This has remained incomplete; that has remained incomplete. What will happen now?' Such thoughts of attachment to worldly things dominate even towards the end of their lives as these are the thoughts that have been dominant throughout their lives. These thoughts of attachment overpower the experience of dying. People miss even this very important last moment of their life which could have taught them a lot of significant things.

A wise person does not lose this invaluable last moment at the time of so-called death. The one who has lived a conscious life and has contemplated over the ultimate aim of human life is eligible for a Supreme Life. He embraces his death with a smile on his lips.

Sam: Is it true that your whole life flashes in front of you just before you die?

Sɪʀsʜʀᴇᴇ: That happens just after so-called death, not just before. Just before death, some thoughts that you have harboured throughout your life flash before your eyes. Understand this through a story.

A man had seven daughters. He spent his entire life facing hardships in the process of earning money to feed and raise them. Now that his daughters had grown up, all his time was being taken up in finding eligible grooms and getting them married. He was pretty sad with his state of affairs. He longed for peace of mind.

Someone informed him about a saint who could help him find peace. He was also warned that the saint would answer only one question. To this, he replied, 'I should get a solution to come out of my meaningless life. How can I experience joy? This is what I am going to ask the saint'. He went to the saint and found him to be young and of marriageable age. The saint asked him, 'What is your question? Why have you come here?' The man could not help but ask, 'Are you married?' The saint replied, 'No. And now you cannot ask another question'.

The man returned home lamenting. Why did this happen with him? He was constantly thinking about finding suitable grooms for his daughters. Therefore, the question just popped out of his mouth. He forgot to ask the right question. He was never able to find peace due to his attachments and obsession.

The problems that you have harboured during your life will crop up in your mind even at the time of your death. It has been seen that whatever people think throughout their lives, they get those same thoughts just before their death. If you have had thoughts of Truth throughout your life, you will have those same thoughts during your death.

Sam: I now understand why you have always emphasised on thinking thoughts of Truth and happy thoughts. So, you were saying that your entire life flashes before you just after you die.

SIRSHREE: Yes. The third question was what happens just

41

after so-called death? That's when the entire film of your life flashes before you. The journey of the subtle body begins after the demise of the gross body. There is a small period of transition before the journey of the subtle body commences, which is called the 'grey period'. During this period, the subtle body recalls its entire physical life. Whatever has happened since childhood till the day of so-called death appears in front of it. It can see in one shot what has happened in its life, and what has not.

When alive, people jump to conclusions all the time whether what has happened until then has been good or bad. Their assessments are usually wrong. You can tell if a movie was good or not, only when you have seen the entire movie. During the grey period, the subtle body is able to see the complete movie of its life. At that time, it is being its own judge. In the grey period, the subtle body sees its complete film, internalises it, gets ready for the life ahead, and continues on its journey.

Sam: What else happens? People believe that you are taken away by angels and exported to a place where you live amidst them.

SIRSHREE: Just after so-called death, angels do not appear to take you to the other world. Nor are you produced in the Court of Heaven in front of God for judgement. These are all figments of imagination made popular by folklore. You will be your own judge and the level of your consciousness will decide your future state and the arrangements for you.

A person suddenly finds himself in an absolutely new environment just after his death. It is like an individual suddenly reaching a new city. He does not know its language. People are new to him. Everything is new to him.

Sam: What happens then?

SIRSHREE: Understand what happens. Understand what happens immediately and what happens long after so-called death – the fourth question.

In this world, when a child is born, doctors and nurses try to ease his entry into this world. They take the best possible care of him. Similarly, there are beings in the other world who help the subtle body make a smooth entry there. Actually, there is no 'there'.

Sam: What do you mean, Sirshree?

SIRSHREE: That world is here itself, it is not far away; it only exists at a different frequency. There are a lot of different kinds of people in that world who render selfless service. Just as we have doctors, nurses, teachers and others serving in this world, there are people who serve the subtle body in its further journey. But what kind of help is given? Help is given to understand the new life and the new environment in order to unlearn their wrong beliefs and notions. They are assisted to clearly understand their false beliefs and misconceptions. Those who learn faster and open up rapidly understand and move forward on the path of progress. Those who are not ready continue to be embroiled in the beliefs of their religion and their deeds, and hence, take time to understand and move on.

This is because the so-called 'holy men' on Earth, in order to fulfil their own vested interests and to keep their business running, have instilled a lot of fears and greed in the minds of people, because of which it is difficult for these people to come out of their beliefs. One such belief is that you will rot in hell if you do not do this, and you will go to heaven if you do that. Such images are deeply embedded in their minds. It is difficult to come out of years of such conditioning.

The beings giving selfless service in the other world will tell the individual, who is now in the subtle world, that there is no such thing like heaven with angels, nor is there any hell with devils who will fry him in scalding oil. As he tries to understand, his mind opens up and he knows that he has to be ready for the journey ahead. He will otherwise be in a dilemma and ask himself, 'What is all this? Why am I not able to understand this? Why is everything so hazy around me? Why can't I see things clearly?'

The more false beliefs and illusions he sheds, the clearer he will be able to see. Otherwise, he will remain in a state of confusion and haze for a long time.

During the grey period, he has seen the entire journey of his physical life. He has seen clearly and completely all that had happened with him. Based on this complete information, he is ready to take the next step easily. Without complete information, he will not be able to move ahead. A man told his friend, 'Whenever I see my grandfather's sword, I am filled with an urge to go to war'. The friend asked, 'Then why don't you join the army?' To this he replied, 'When I think about joining the army, I also see my grandfather's amputated leg'. Thus, if you have complete information, you can take the right decisions. People cannot take correct decisions because of lack of information or incomplete information.

There are people in Part Two who are always ready to help you out. They will guide and mentor you; just as you see saints and noble men guiding people on this Earth. They are guiding people who are confused, troubled and embroiled in myriad thoughts and beliefs.

Just as we have hospitals on Earth, likewise there are hospitals in that world too, although of a different kind. People there do not experience diseases or pains of the physical body that can be cured with medicines. This is simply because they do not have a physical body anymore. Hence, the hospitals there are of a different kind.

Sam: What kind of hospitals are there?

Sɪʀsʜʀᴇᴇ: The word 'hospital' is being used here as a metaphor only and not in the actual sense. Grasp the meaning underlying the words rather than getting entangled in words. The subtle body will continue on its journey and will understand that all physical pains have disappeared, but it is experiencing other types of problems now. And then based on its level of consciousness, it will live in Part Two on a particular plane.

Sam: I did not understand.

Sirshree: Let us assume a man journeyed (he died) to Part Two. What is his level of consciousness? Is it at the highest level or at the bottom? If his consciousness is at the lower levels, he is allowed entry only to the lower sub-planes, where he will be living with people of his level. He is denied access to the higher levels. He cannot bribe anyone to gain access to the higher levels like some people do here on Earth to enter exotic places. The understanding that he has gained in his life here is his only passport there.

A wonderful aspect of the journey of the subtle body in the subtle world is that people with the same ideology, similar thinking patterns, and similar dispositions live together. On this Earth, people living under the same roof have different thinking patterns and dispositions. Everybody has different ideas, which causes a lot of problems. Hence, many-a-time, people have to stay together against each others' wishes.

But this is fine because the Earth is a practice ground for us to prepare for our long journey in Part Two. You may say that here in Part One, heaven and hell exist at the same place. A home can be heaven or hell at different times. When it is filled with peace and harmony, it is like heaven. When it is filled with conflicts and hatred, it becomes hell. A house where people with negative thoughts live is like hell. Others don't like to visit that house as they feel uncomfortable in it. A temple can be like heaven, but even hell at times. When terrorists enter a temple, it becomes hell. A shop can be both heaven and hell. When a nasty person is managing the shop, it becomes hell; customers avoid entering it. On the other hand, when someone pleasant is managing the same shop, it becomes heaven. People prefer to shop there only when the pleasant one is present. They avoid it when the first person is around as his behaviour is not good.

However, the beauty of the subtle world is that people of the same thinking live together. People, who do not fit, get shunted to other levels automatically.

Sam: That's wonderful! But how does that happen?

Sirshree: Understand this with an example:

There is a bungalow having seven rooms. One room is completely dark, the other is lit by a candle, the third is illuminated with a bulb, and the fourth has a tube light. Which of these rooms would you

47

like to live in? Of course, you would like to go into the room in which you will feel comfortable. Some people like to eat in candlelight; they will go in the room lit by candles. Some like the feel of the tube light, some like the brightness of the bulb, and there are others who like to sit in the dark. Everyone chooses a room according to his liking and comfort.

In the same way, people in the subtle world choose their surroundings according to their ideology and level of consciousness. The higher and purer your thoughts are, the higher will be the levels you keep reaching. You will continue to rise higher.

Sam: What happens with bad and evil people? And what happens with good people?

SIRSHREE: If a person has lived a greedy and selfish life on Earth, he finds himself in a hazy, dark, gloomy, miserable, and heavy atmosphere in the other world, which is ruled by fear and suffering. He has difficulty understanding that he has died. If he does not come out of his ignorance soon, then, according to the rules of the other world, he has to descend to even lower sub-planes, where the level of consciousness is still lower. He finds himself in a far darker and miserable world.

If the person who has died has been violent, greedy and self-centred on Earth, he will be surrounded by similar people in the next world. There is an atmosphere of darkness and hopelessness around him. If, even in these surroundings, he does not regret his mistakes, then he reaches still lower sub-planes where it is even darker. When he is inspired to rise higher in life, someone reaches out to help him, provided he asks for guidance with a feeling of surrender and not egotism.

If a man's life on Earth has been that of patience, selfless service and empathy for others, the other world presents him with a life full of love, joy and beauty.

Long after so-called death, you will get a role to play there which will be your future course of action or goal. You will perform that role out of sheer bliss. Right now, the roles that we play have an ulterior motive to back them – earning money, self-gratification, fulfilling physical desires, etc. But there you will play your role out of happiness and as an expression of Self.

But let us talk about your role and goal in this life. What do you think is the purpose of life, Sameer? Before you meet Sirshree again to understand more details of Part Two, contemplate on one key question: how will your life be transformed now that you have understood what happens before and after death?

Sam: Yes, Sirshree. I will contemplate on this.

SIRSHREE: Thank you for the opportunity of serving you.

Doubts – What the Hell!

As Sameer walked out, he felt elated. He had begun to understand something beautiful. He was looking forward to the following Wednesday to meet Sirshree again. But, the very next day, some doubts started creeping in.

The questions and doubts were like a storm that grew bigger with every passing day. Sameer knew this would happen. Sirshree had warned him against it. The puzzle was scrambled and annoyingly complicated. Being analytical by nature and having been in the software industry for many years, critical thinking came naturally to him. He checked for defects in the wisdom.

Is this all true? Where is the evidence that it is true? What does scientific research and other literature on death say? Are these merely words for comfort?

By the time he was to meet Sirshree again, he was stung, wounded and defeated. Finally, he knocked on Sirshree's door, waiting to challenge him.

SIRSHREE: Sameer, what is it that you want to challenge today?

Sam: How did you know, Sirshree?!

SIRSHREE: Sirshree also knows that you haven't contemplated on the significance of the knowledge of Part Two in Part One, as told to you last time.

Sam: You are amazing. How can you read my mind?

SIRSHREE: When you transcend the mind, you can predict every move the mind makes. The self-stabilised use their mind and can intuitively read others' minds. But there is no magic in it. It is unfortunate that many people believe that on being stabilised in self-realisation, one acquires magical powers. This is a myth. It's just that knowing the nature of the mind becomes plain and simple.

Sam: This is why I like your teachings and your books. You have always clearly espoused reality and exposed myths. But this matter about death – it's a bit too much. I wish to ask you on what basis you say what happens after death? I can't believe it just like that!

SIRSHREE: There are five foundations based on which Sirshree speaks about life after death. But, before we come to that, tell me, what research have you done on this so as to not believe or believe?

Sam: Err...actually none. I don't know much on this topic. I haven't done any research.

SIRSHREE: That's the point. What books have you read on this topic? Whom have you met regarding this? What have you read about the latest scientific develop-

ments such as Krillion photography that shows you
the energy body? Then, how can you say that you
cannot believe it? What is your research based on
which you say that you don't believe it?

Sam: I get the point, Sirshree. Before coming to meet
you again, I shall do some research. At least, some
preliminary research.

SIRSHREE: Coming back to your question, there are five foundations based on which Sirshree states that there is
life after death. The first foundation is that science
has proven today that everything is just energy
consisting of frequencies and vibrations. Earlier,
it was believed that everything was matter. Today,
frequencies and vibrations have been understood
with the help of certain instruments. The second
foundation is the NDE Foundation.

Sam: Are you referring to near-death experiences when
you say NDE?

SIRSHREE: Yes. This second basis consists of those people
who returned to life after being declared dead by
the doctors. The experiences they narrated have
been recorded and are termed as 'near-death
experiences'. A majority of them had remarkably
similar experiences. Those pieces have been put
together to understand life after death.

The third source is the ascetics and yogis who
have practised rigorous physical and mental
discipline for years and through their immense
concentration have attained supernatural powers.

Due to these powers, they have realised that our subtle body can go out of our gross body and come back. The testimony provided by these ascetics endowed with supernatural powers serves as the third foundation.

Sam: Are you referring to astral travel here?

SIRSHREE: Astral travel too. Then the fourth basis is the great saints who have realised the Self, or in other words, have attained enlightenment. Lord Buddha, Lord Mahavira, Adi Shankaracharya, Guru Nanak, Saint Dnyaneshwar, Jesus Christ, Prophet Mohammad are just a few of those who have known their real Self. Acquiring supernatural powers is one thing and self-realisation quite another. The knowledge attained after self-realisation is the fourth basis.

Sam: I have faith in you, Sirshree. I know you are sta-bilised in the Self. I have experienced the Self in your retreats. I am certain about my progress towards self-stabilisation with you. Hence, this is the foundation that helps me to not reject the no-tion of life after death completely. But the other foundations you mentioned are also beginning to make sense.

SIRSHREE: It shall not only make sense to you, something else will also happen.

Sam: What, Sirshree?

SIRSHREE: You shall see one day. The fifth foundation is the experiences of those who, after some accident, are able to hear voices which others cannot hear, or see subtle bodies that normal people are not able to see. Taking them through rigorous tests, scientists had to accept that they were not suffering from hallucinations or mental disorders, instead they were able to fully utilise the power of their brains, which normal people cannot.

Sam: I cannot digest this.

SIRSHREE: You should believe or not believe only after you have contemplated on the topic. Understand what to believe, how to believe, and what interferes in believing, through this short story:

There was a scientist who was utterly terrified of death. To deceive death, he created ten clones of himself. It took him ten years to make them. The day the Lord of Death came to take him, he saw eleven look-alikes standing in front of him. The Lord of Death said, 'The person who has made these clones has done a perfect job, except for one mistake'. On hearing this, the scientist could not contain himself and blurted out, "Absolutely not!" The Lord of Death replied, 'This' is the mistake you have done! You could not suppress your ego. If you had put this ego in the rest of the clones, I would not have been able to single you out. Only 'you' have this ego. None of the replicas have it. Otherwise, everyone would have responded saying, "Absolutely not!" Only you said so and hence you are caught'.

What is the difference between a human, an animal and an object? Humans have an 'ego' –

the feeling of 'I', 'me', 'mine'. Animals have a simple or instinctive mind without any 'I' feeling. Objects just have vibrations. It is thoughts that distinguish a human from other creations and makes him supreme.

However, the thought of 'I' gives rise to the fear of death in humans. The thought 'I will die' leaves humans in the shadow of death. What we consider as death is actually the death of thoughts. What happens at night in deep sleep? What happens to a person in coma? In both, the experience is similar to the experience of death. Thoughts are non-existent or dead in a body during the state of deep sleep or coma. In one case, thoughts are dead for eight hours, and in the other, maybe for days or months. A person considers the death of the feeling of 'I' or 'me' as his own death. In reality, it is just that the thoughts have stopped arising; which is wrongly taken as death. The thought of 'I' is the ego that leads man to think of himself as a separate entity. Otherwise, the world is a single unit. Trees, mountains, animals, humans, birds, objects – all are parts of the same single unit, even though they appear to be totally different from each other. It is like the fingers which look different but are joined to the same hand. Similarly, the entire world is like the hand of God.

In the example of the scientist, the feeling of ego resulted in the fear of death in his mind. He wasted precious time creating replicas of himself when he could have created something useful.

The scientist, in fact, had made two mistakes. The first mistake was that he spent ten years to make ten clones of himself. If he had spent those years understanding what life after death is, he would not have feared death and not wasted so much time. The second mistake he committed was that he kept on fleeing from death instead of trying to find the truth about it.

Sam: How very subtly you have highlighted my mistakes! I get that I have spent enough time for my aspirations, for my business. And the second mistake is that I am fleeing from death instead of trying to find the truth about it, and am resisting the truth even when you are presenting it to me.

SIRSHREE: This happens with many people. But we should be ready to listen when we have the opportunity to gain such profound knowledge.

Sam: I totally agree that I am very fortunate to receive such profound knowledge from you. I cannot thank you enough for that. In addition, Sirshree, you have made this topic so easy to understand and accept since it corroborates with science too.

SIRSHREE: But remember that the truth is not science alone. What does science have to say about the body and the consciousness that is within the body? Science has its own parameters as it breaks up everything into small parts and then examines each part. Science is not complete in itself. Yet, Sameer, do read what you can and apply your scientific mind and tell Sirshree if it corroborates with this knowledge or not.

This Earth is full of visual scenes, voices, smells, tastes and a lot of various things, but science states that everything is one and the same, just consisting of different frequencies. For instance, water, ice and vapour are different forms of the same thing. The different forms are brought about by the changes in frequency of the same basic substratum. Science today is realising that there is just one basic energy form which vibrates everywhere. If this is so, then the body that we possess is also made up of vibrations. This body ranges from the gross body to the subtle body.

The question 'Is there life after death?' is as profound as the question 'Does God exist?' Some people believe in the existence of God and some do not. But the question that has to be asked of them is whether they have done any kind of research on this question, or is it all based on hearsay?

An atheist should be asked whether he does not believe in God just because some of his prayers have not been answered, or because some of his prayers have not been answered in the way he wanted. Most people stop believing in God when they don't get what they had prayed for. This is not seeking; this is ego.

On the other hand, there is a person who believes in God but has never done any research on it. He blindly accepts all those answers that have been handed over to him since childhood.

Those who really seek the answer to the above question realise that the question of whether God exists or not is in itself a wrong question. God alone exists. The question is, do 'you' really exist?

When you ask a person who is lying on the bed with eyes closed, 'Are you awake?', if he says 'Yes', you know that he is awake. If he says 'No', even then you know that he is awake; otherwise how could he have answered? Likewise, when people are asked, 'Is there God?', then whether they say yes or no, it does not change the fact that there is God. Their existence is proof of the existence of God. When a person begins to know the real Self, all the secrets begin to unfold before him.

Similarly, Sirshree asks that if you do not believe in life after death, have you done any research on it? Honestly ask yourself this question. Do not lead your life based on unsubstantiated beliefs. Live with an open mind and seek with a thirst for knowledge.

Sam: I apologise for my foolishness. I neither con-templated on what you said, nor did I do any research.

SIRSHREE: Contemplate. Do some research. Only then will you be ready to receive the final answer. There can be three answers to every question. It has to be borne in mind that the answers given here are according to the circumstances of the world today and as per your level of understanding and in contemporary language. These are not the final answers. Answers change according to the stage or level of understanding of the seeker. You should ask yourself whether you are ready to listen to the real and final answer. It is essential to contemplate on this because some people ask questions just to confirm their existing knowledge and beliefs. If the answers match their beliefs, they say, 'We already knew this and it tallies with the answers we know. Hence, this proves that we knew the right thing'. If they get an answer that does not conform to their notions, then their faith begins to waver.

Sam: What are the three levels of answers, Sirshree?

SIRSHREE: Every spiritual question has at least three answers. The first kind is the superficial or preliminary answer. These are given to a novice who does not know much about the subject and is not really prepared to listen. Preliminary answers are meant for them.

The second kind of answer is given to that person who has some knowledge and has done some contemplation.

The third kind of answer is given to those who have gained maturity or understanding of life. They have gained maturity through satsang, by listening to discourses, through contemplation and meditation. They can understand the final answer.

Even if they do not understand the answer, they will contemplate upon it; they will not abandon its pursuit easily. If the new answers do not match their ideas, they will still not discard them.

So, Sameer, also contemplate on what level of answers you are prepared for and come back next week. Thank you for the opportunity of serving you.

A Death Search

Sameer relied on the Internet as his main source of research. He contemplated on what Sirshree had revealed to him thus far. He also contemplated on what level of answer he was prepared for. Some evidence he found on the net matched perfectly to what Sirshree said. But, when there was a mismatch, questions and doubts sprang up. Then a thought came to him that the teachings of the Buddha, Christ and others that he was reading up on were documented long after they were gone. Is it possible that these were not accurate? It occurred to him, 'What am I testing Sirshree's knowledge against? Do I trust the Internet more than a living, enlightened guru?'

He opened his eyes. He was in the meditation room where he had arrived one hour earlier for his appointment with Sirshree. The room was serene, the walls were sea blue and at the back of the room was a huge picture of Mother Earth. A few people sat alongside, waiting their turn. Like them, Sameer too waited eagerly.

Sam: Sirshree, thank you for the last meeting. I realise that I had not come with an open mind. But I am more prepared now. I also want to clarify that I am ready for the second level of answers and wish to be at the third level; but you are a better judge of whether I have progressed spiritually enough.

SIRSHREE: Okay. So, what did you do during the last week?

Sam: The first thing I did was to read about near-death experiences. A lot of people have expressed their views on life after death on the Internet and in books. Many people who have had near-death experiences have recorded their statements. These people are of different nationalities and speak different languages. Their experiences are, however, very similar. I read a fascinating news article on BBC news, in which scientists investigating near-death experiences say that they have found evidence to suggest that consciousness can continue to exist after the brain has ceased to function.

The researchers interviewed sixty-three patients who had survived heart attacks. These interviews were done within a week of their attacks. Out of the total sixty-three patients, fifty-six had no recollection of the period of unconsciousness they experienced while, effectively, clinically dead. However, seven had some memories, four of which were counted as near-death experiences. They described feelings of peace and joy, time speeding up, heightened senses, losing awareness of body, seeing a bright light, entering another world, encountering a mystical being and coming to 'a point of no return'.

SIRSHREE: Hmmm…what else did you find?

Sam: I then studied astral travel. I found it fascinating
           as well. Because of your warning, I did not restrict
           my study to just astral travel. I spoke to five people
           who have had out-of-body experiences. One of
           them had an out-of-body experience suddenly.
           Two had the experience in a spiritual retreat.
           One had it during a hypnosis session. Another
           had learnt to do astral travel. This was the most
           fascinating part. They all reported about leaving
           their physical body and seeing it from outside.
           Some talked about seeing their physical body from
           above. Some talked about even wandering out
           of their house. I was so taken in by this subject,
           that I wanted to ask you how I can grow spiritual
           enough to experience it.

SIRSHREE: There is nothing spiritual about it. It is a power
          of the body. If you build your muscles and learn
          the skill and art of body building, do you say it
          is a spiritual experience?

Sam: No. But doesn't the word 'spiritual' arise from the
           word 'spirit'?

SIRSHREE: Yes, but a spiritual experience is when you feel
          oneness with the universe. There is no out-of-
          body experience in that, but more of a 'one-body'
          experience. It can be said to be a 'soulful' expe-
          rience. It happens when you are in touch with
          the 'fifth'.

Sam: With the blissful sheath, with the one who dons

63

the gross and the subtle body – the Self?

SIRSHREE: Yes. Satori experiences or oneness experiences or a Self-realisation experience that thousands have experienced in Tej Gyan retreats happen when the Self returns to Itself. This means when the body-mind mechanism, which is the combination of the gross and subtle body or four sheaths, is used as a medium for the Self to experience Itself. This is akin to deep sleep. But the difference is that you are aware during this experience. This is important. This is a soulful experience. This is a true spiritual experience. Out-of-body experiences or astral travel or even awakening of the kundalini energy are all to do with mere powers of the body-mind. Sameer, Sirshree recommends you to not indulge in all those things.

Sam: Oh, but I thought Sirshree would be pleased with my interest.

SIRSHREE: Focus on the desire to attain the Supreme Truth with understanding, not on increasing the powers of the body or attaining siddhis or learning astral travelling. All of these ultimately result in the ego becoming stronger. And until the ego drops, the Self does not shine.

Sam: I get your point, Sirshree. Thank you for your candid and clear feedback. I now understand how easily the mind can get swayed into interesting but unwanted things in the name of research and seeking the knowledge of life after death.

By studying near-death experiences and astral travel, I have begun to understand what happens just before death and what happens just after. But I still cannot fathom the answer to the other two questions. My final part of research was turning to religions and saints. I looked up the Internet and found what many highly evolved souls have said. I was amazed that it resonates so much with what you said. And now I understand what they say as well. I have brought a collection of these quotations.

SIRSHREE: You may read them.

Sam: They may be a bit long. When I was writing these quotations down from books or from the net, wherever words such as 'after life' or 'other side' were used, I substituted them with 'subtle world'. I have done similar conversions when it came to the gross body or subtle body. Thus, these notes are more for my understanding.

SIRSHREE: Don't worry, it's your understanding that Sirshree wants to see. If something is grossly wrong with what you quote, Sirshree shall point it out.

Sam: That is great. The first set of quotations is about the gross and subtle bodies.

1) When saints and yogis, who have higher levels of consciousness, leave their gross body, they continue their journey at the highest level (or plane) of the subtle world. They become instrumental for giving special guidance to people

at every level. They are recognised much more over there as compared to on Earth.

2) When the gross body perishes with the blow of death, the subtle body remains and prevents consciousness from merging with the Supreme Consciousness in the state of awareness.

3) When a person dreams, he is in his subtle body, and just like subtle beings, he is able to create anything effortlessly in his dreams.

4) The subtle body experiences agelessness in the other world. It does not experience the development of wrinkles, old age, feebleness of the senses or weakness of the body with the passage of time.

5) A person retains the same consciousness, knowledge and understanding he had throughout his life, after death. He retains in the subtle body the same doubting and calculative mind. His conduct, thinking and tendencies as in the gross body also remain the same.

6) Subtle bodies can experience touch, smell, flavour, appearance and words through their intuition. They can even experience the smell, flavour and touch of light.

SIRSHREE: As far as the first quote is concerned, not just saints and yogis, but everyone continues their journey. However, those at a higher level of consciousness in Part One continue at a higher level of consciousness in Part Two as well. As far as the third quote is concerned, when you dream, you can have an out-of-body experience. But saying that when you are dreaming, you are in your subtle body, may not be entirely correct.

Sam: Thanks for the clarification, Sirshree. Shall I resume my reading?

SIRSHREE: Yes, please do.

Sam: The second set of quotes relates to comparison between Part One and Part Two.

1) The degrees, titles, position, status, power and wealth acquired on Earth end with the death of the gross body. All these have no meaning in the subtle world. Purity of the heart, love and compassion are the qualities that count in that world. With these feelings within, you can rise higher. You are recognised there based on these qualities.

2) As compared to Earth, the subtle world runs much more smoothly, naturally, and with the simple or instinctive mind according to God's wish and divine scheme. While there are continuous wars and violence on Earth, life goes on peacefully in the subtle world. There is equality and harmony among all.

3) The subtle world is infinitely beautiful, pure, clean and orderly. The terrestrial blemishes present on the Earth such as micro-organisms, insects, snakes, weeds, etc. are not present in that world. Unlike the variable climates and

seasons of the Earth, the subtle world maintains an even temperature of an eternal spring.

4) A person is liberated from tiredness, old age and lethargy of the body in his subtle form. His mental laziness and inertia, however, remain the same in the subtle body as it was in the physical body. Therefore, we have to get rid of this inertia and dullness on Earth.

5) The subtle world is not a place amidst the stars far away from Earth. It exists in the space surrounding the Earth. It is made up of subtle or fine vibrations of light energy and colours and is hundreds of times bigger than the gross world (the Earth). It can be imagined like a huge balloon (the subtle world) with a small basket (the gross world) attached underneath.

SIRSHREE: The last quote is important to understand. The description in the last quote is imaginary. But it is important to understand that everything is here and now. Part Two is present right here and now, just at another frequency.

As far as the comparison between Part One and Part Two is concerned, though Part Two is much more smooth, note that universal laws operate in Part One too.

Sam: Thanks for pointing it out. Life here is organised chaos (*smiles*). I did have one question about the life there. What about money? Will I work there too? What about travel?

SIRSHREE: There is no such thing like money in that world. Hence, there is no need to do any business or job there. A business or job is carried out on Earth to gratify oneself, because you have to satisfy your physical cravings. When the physical body has dissipated, where is the need for money? All troubles which have their root in money vanish. Today, in more than 90 per cent of the cases, most activities that you engage in are directed towards making money.

However, there is a new kind of life in Part Two. People converse through telepathy or mental communication. If you want, you can speak, but it is not required because people can read each others' thoughts very clearly. No one can fool the other by thinking one thing and saying something else. There, it is not possible to say 'I love you' from outside, but mean 'I hate you' from inside. This cannot happen in Part Two because 'thought' is the biggest power in that world. Part Two or the subtle world is based on the fundamental principle of thought. You can reach a particular place instantly just by thinking about that place. This is not possible on Earth as there are limitations of the physical or external body. Here, you have to move with your physical body. You could have otherwise just thought about a place, and lo, you would have been there.

All activities there happen on the basis of thoughts because thought is the power of that world and the governing principle. That is why Sirshree usually emphasises the importance of 'happy thoughts' in his teachings. You will understand the importance of happy thoughts in your life here, more in Part Two. According to the level of understanding that you have gained here, you will be able to experience bliss a thousand-fold in that world.

Sam: The third set of quotes is actually about the power of thoughts and its relation to the planes of consciousness in the subtle world.

SIRSHREE: Go on, read them.

Sam: 1) A person cannot enter the plane of highest consciousness in the subtle world until he makes a successful transition from *Savikalpa* samadhi state [samadhi reached with the aid of a mantra, breathing, etc.] to *Nirvikalpa* samadhi state [a deep state of samadhi which is reached without any aid or support].

2) People with higher levels of consciousness live in the higher sub-planes of the subtle world. Most people of Earth have to pass through different sub-planes of consciousness. Only those who have annihilated their tendencies and bad habits of the subtle body can go directly to the higher sub-plane.

3) There are different levels of spherical sub-planes for the higher and lower subtle bodies. The subtle bodies with noble thoughts that reside at the higher sub-planes are not confined

to any part of the subtle world and can travel anywhere they wish. However, the lower subtle bodies have limited areas where they can move about. In this gross world, humans stay on the surface of the Earth, worms in the soil, fish in water and birds in the sky. Similarly, different areas are allocated to different subtle bodies in the subtle world.

4) In the subtle world, everyone has to learn to control his desires and channelise them in the right direction at some point of time. The more you have worked upon exercising control over your desires on Earth, the more you benefit in the subtle world.

5) The more the desires and wants that man carries into the subtle world, the worse is the life he leads at the lower sub-planes.

6) Whatever a human can do in his imagination is what a subtle being can do in reality. The subtle beings at the higher sub-planes of consciousness have supreme freedom. They can manifest into reality any of their thoughts without performing any activity and without any bondage of *karmas* or deeds.

SIRSHREE: About the quote on samadhi, you have read that the transition to higher planes cannot be made until samadhi has been mastered. One clarification there – samadhi is just one of the ways.

Sam: So, how does one go to the higher planes or upper

levels? What happens exactly on those higher planes of consciousness?

SIRSHREE: Those who are filled with love, compassion, selfless service and patience on this Earth reach the higher sub-planes in Part Two, depending on the degree of purity of their mind. The atmosphere there is bright, clean, beautiful and blissful. When they interact with people in that world, they expand their knowledge further, due to which they are able to perceive and understand the highest expression of the Self.

Selfless love, kindness and compassion are given the highest value in the subtle world. These are not given as much importance on Earth. People on Earth adopt these qualities just to impress others or to get their work done. But these qualities count the most in the higher sub-planes of the other world. As people become more selfless, they find themselves at higher sub-planes. This is true progress.

Upon encountering the truth in the other world, people wonder if they are the ones who are dead or it is the people on Earth who are living under such a huge illusion. Every person in Part Two begins to understand the importance of love and peace. Music, art, colours, creativity are the forms of expression in that world, although it is difficult to convey their real meaning in the language of this world.

On this Earth we have three dimensions – length,

breadth and height. In the other world, other than these three, there is a fourth dimension, which has never been expressed in our language. That is why we do not have those words in our vocabulary.

No one can be cheated or misunderstood in that world. People act mostly on the basis of their intuition.

If, in the physical world, someone were to introduce a law that says you can go and stay anywhere on Earth, you will not be punished for it; you can murder anyone, you can steal, you can cheat and you will never be punished, what will happen? Those who are good and honest will come together. Likewise, those who cheat and murder will form their own groups. This grouping will occur spontaneously. In the same way, people form their own groups according to their level of consciousness in Part Two.

Sameer, tell me one thing. Why doesn't everybody steal on Earth?

Sam: Because people are honest.

Sɪʀsʜʀᴇᴇ: True. But, a lot of people do not steal, not because they are honest, but because of the fear of being caught and punished. They have been holding themselves from stealing only because of the fear of punishment.

In Part Two, birds of a feather will definitely flock together. Thieves will group with thieves. Good people will find their own company. Those who are pure, true and childlike from within, will live with people like themselves. Those who pretend to be good will group with similar people. No one can be deceived in that world. Bad people will not be able to interfere or dictate the lives of good people. This is the best aspect of the other world.

With the subtle body, all physical constraints are done away with. People with bad tendencies get separated from good-natured people. People of a bad nature do not enter the area where people with pure thoughts live as they do not feel comfortable there. For example, someone who likes to stay in a dark room does not like to go into a room which is full of bright lights. And even if he does enter that room, he will be relieved to come back in his familiar surroundings. We always like to go where we feel comfortable.

Sam: I understand better now. And speaking about company in Part Two, the next set of quotes is about communication in the subtle world.

SIRSHREE: Please continue.

Sam: 1) In the subtle world, whatever thoughts you bring into your mind or whatever thoughts arise in your mind due to your nature get actualised instantly. That means, in the subtle form you can acquire any object you want just by wishing for it. This is because there the power of thoughts acts instantly, whereas on Earth it takes some time for your thoughts to turn into reality.

2) People in the subtle world communicate with each other through astral television or telepathy. Therefore, no miscommunications or confusions arise because of spoken and written words as in the physical state.

3) A person completely loses all the external flashiness or 'personality' on entering the subtle world. The real appearance, as the person is from his heart, comes to the fore. We cannot put up a façade to impress others in the subtle state as we can in our physical state.

4) There can be minor changes in the external appearance of the subtle body during its transition from the gross state to the subtle state. In spite of that, the subtle body with its accurate intuition power can easily recognise its old relatives located at various planes of consciousness. And it can also welcome its relatives when they enter the subtle world.

5) People who know each other in the physical world can easily recognise each other in their subtle form too. While on Earth, pain is felt at the time of physical death of a dear one due to the assumption that love is of transient nature. This pain is dissolved in the subtle form when the loved ones reunite and feel elated on experiencing the eternal nature of love.

6) The people in the subtle world do not have any connection with people on Earth. People in the subtle world can appear or

disappear as they wish. Subtle bodies look mostly like their physical bodies but they have the freedom to adopt any form they want. They can communicate with each other with ease and can recognise each other in any form, just as you can recognise your favourite movie star in any disguise.

SIRSHREE: As far as the last quote goes, saying that the beings in Part Two don't have any connection with the beings in Part One is not correct. Understand that the role of some people both in Part One and Part Two is to communicate with both these worlds.

Sam: So, that is where mediums come in. I always wondered how they worked.

SIRSHREE: Yes. But not all mediums are genuine. Nevertheless, it is the role of some bodies to communicate between these worlds. Okay, what else have you got?

Sam: The last set of quotes is the most intriguing. I couldn't quite grasp them fully. They are about what happens afterwards, such as heaven or reincarnation.

1) Death and rebirth are mere thoughts in the world of highest consciousness. People there thrive only on ever new ambrosia of wisdom. They drink from the fountains of peace, walk on the space-less surface of the experience of Being, and take dips in the sea of Supreme Bliss.

2) Just as great people are sent to Earth to guide

mortals in their karmas or deeds in the physical world, similarly some saints, after having provided guidance on Earth, have the possibility of working as guides in the higher sub-planes of the subtle world.

3) In the world of highest consciousness, many beings reside for thousands of years. Then, through deep meditation, their consciousness becomes free and releases itself from the causal sheath and attains the pinnacle of Supreme Consciousness.

4) The great one, who attains the pinnacle of Supreme Consciousness, can either choose to be born on Earth to show people the path to God, or act as a guide to the beings entering the subtle world.

SIRSHREE: The mention of the possibility of working as a guide on the higher sub-planes in one of the quotes is quite correct. But the phrase 'people are sent to Earth' may be construed wrongly. People are not sent to Earth. Only memories are used.

Sam: I did not understand this answer. And this thing about reincarnation and rebirth is what baffles me the most.

SIRSHREE: Since today's time is running out, we shall take up this topic next time. But contemplate on the original question Sirshree asked.

Sam: (sheepishly) I don't remember it, Sirshree.

SIRSHREE: (smiling) Contemplate on the significance of knowing about life after death. Why should you know this now? Why did Sirshree bring up this topic in response to your initial question about feeling a vacuum in your life? Sirshree is happy about the research you have done. But Sirshree will still be unhappy if you die today. Why?

Sam: Ha ha... I have begun to see why already. I shall surely contemplate and come back, Sirshree.

Sɪʀsʜʀᴇᴇ: And we shall take up your questions on the last set of quotes – on heaven and rebirth. May you be reborn in this life itself, Sameer. That is my blessing for you. Thank you for the opportunity of serving you.

Death Rites

'May you be reborn in this birth itself'. These words echoed in Sameer's mind throughout the week. He contemplated on the significance of Sirshree's teachings on life after death.

On Saturday evening, Sameer got a phone call. His father's brother, who had been a general in the army, had died in a helicopter mishap. Since Sameer was his only surviving relative, he was informed that the body would be flown in and handed over to him by Sunday evening.

Sameer was not very attached to his uncle. He had met him on very few occasions. The last time Sameer had seen him was during his father's demise. His uncle had flown in and then breezed out of the funeral. Now it was time for Sameer to perform his uncle's last rites.

Since Sameer had only twenty-four hours left for the impending last rites, he called Sirshree's staff for an appointment the next day. He knew that Sirshree usually did not meet seekers as regularly as he was meeting him. Weekly appointments with him were an exceptional case. Hence, he hesitatingly asked if it would be possible *to meet Sirshree to get some guidance on his uncle's death. He said that he knew that Sirshree spent a lot of time on Sunday, meeting seekers who had attended his retreats and guiding them through open question-and-answer sessions. However, he entreated the staff to see what could be done. They told him they would call back in an hour, but it would be best if he could meet Sirshree on Wednesday as planned. They asked him if he was in grief over the death. Sameer said that he was not. He just wanted some guidance and it would be alright if an appointment was not possible on Sunday.*

To his surprise, he got a call back in fifteen minutes and was told that he could meet Sirshree before the question-and-answer session on Sunday. The next day, he could not stop thinking about how his uncle's journey to Part Two would have progressed.

Sam: Thank you for meeting me at such short notice. I'm surprised that you agreed to meet me so fast.

Sirshree: Every scene is a preparation for the next scene. There is a special reason why you are being given this knowledge. So, what was the urgency?

Sam: The reason I am meeting you today is that my uncle, my father's brother, died yesterday. I am responsible for his last rites today evening. The reason I wanted to meet you was to seek your guidance on the same. Having been under your tutelage, I have come to dislike all rituals and superstition. I was wondering what to do this evening. Plus I wanted to know if these rituals would have any bearing on the planes of consciousness one attains in Part Two.

SIRSHREE: There are many rituals. Which rituals are you referring to?

Sam: I have seen Hindu, Christian and Islamic rituals. I have read about Jewish and Tibetan Buddhist rituals. One can say that all rituals across religions and sects boil down to one of these three types of rites. First, the body is consigned to the flames or buried depending upon the religion of the deceased. Second, mourning meetings are held for the departed. Third, certain rituals and prayers are done on the third or thirteenth day after death. Is there any logic behind these? I have always logically rejected them. Having now understood that the journey continues, I wanted to know whether these rituals impact the subtle body.

SIRSHREE: You have mentioned three types of rituals. Now, there are three reasons why any of these rituals are performed. The first reason is that these rituals are performed as a precaution for the health of people in the house. The room in which the dead body has been kept is cleaned so that others do not get infected by the disease that the dead person had. The micro-organisms that might develop in the dead body are gotten rid of.

Sam: Well, that seems logical.

SIRSHREE: Yes. Any ritual carried out with understanding is fine. The second reason for performing these rites is so that the subtle body should commence its journey ahead as soon as possible. It should not continue to be attached to its gross body. That is why the gross body is consigned to the flames or buried. Performing this rite is absolutely essential. When the subtle body realises that its gross body has been destroyed, it becomes ready for its journey ahead. The greatest revelation for the subtle body is that although it was thinking, 'I am dying,' it has not actually died. It is amazed. It is also confused because the more beliefs it carries, the more confusion it experiences in its new life. It cannot make out if it is hallucinating or dreaming, whether it is dead or alive.

Sam: So, the subtle body continues to watch over the gross body after death? Will it also happen in your case when your body dies?

Sirshree: If one has the wisdom of what happens in Part Two then the subtle body is not as attached to the gross body. The whole experience of the rituals may even seem amusing to some wise subtle bodies. Thus, this ritual is not required in all cases. But for most people, sending out a signal to the subtle body helps. Understand this through an example.

You must have watched murder mystery movies, wherein detectives try to nab the killer. A lot of investigation and search goes on. At the end of the chase, people realise that the murder, for which the killer is being chased, has not taken place at all. The person whose death was being investigated is very much alive. He is hale and hearty. You might have seen such movies. The film that seemed to have suspense and mystery turns out to be a farce or a comedy.

Similarly, in some subtle bodies, the whole incident of death may seem to be a farce or a comedy – that it is alive, only its gross body is gone. It is feeling or experiencing in the same way as it was before death. Therefore, it is important to perform the last rites so that the subtle body gets on with its onward journey without any delay.

Sam: And what is the third reason, Sirshree?

Sɪʀsʜʀᴇᴇ: The third reason behind performing these rituals after death is to help the relatives and near and dear ones to come out of their own fears. Thus, some of the rites that people perform after a death are, in fact, done for themselves. They fear that the one who is dead should not resurface in any other form. Hence, they perform rites and rituals to mitigate any such possibility.

Some people feel guilty or scared that they might not have behaved well with the departed. They perform the rituals to pacify the departed soul so that it does not continue to be miserable or appear before them to make them miserable. They do certain things to eliminate their fears such as feeding cows or feeding the deceased person's favourite food to holy men. They perform some kind of ceremonies in order to get rid of fear and guilt from their hearts.

Sam: What is Sirshree's recommendation? Should

rituals be performed or not? And if so, which rituals would you recommend?

SIRSHREE: Different kinds of rituals are performed after death in different religions. What is important is the intention behind performing them. If a ceremony is being held in order to feed a number of people, certainly go ahead and do it. If you are carrying out the ritual to pay respect to the departed, then do it by all means. But your efforts will be in vain if you think that you are feeding the departed since the departed soul may be hungry. This means that if you believe that all those offerings you make to cows or priests will reach the departed, then you are wrong. Those who have died have been liberated from physical needs. They have no need for food or money. They do not need food to survive in the other world.

So, if you are performing any rituals after somebody's death, ask yourself the intention behind it. Rituals done to cleanse the environment, to give a message to the subtle body to continue its journey without clinging to life on Earth, to help people here in Part One to be rid of negative emotions – are all helpful. Again, they are not absolutely necessary but are helpful. The intention behind the rites is more important.

Sam: Excellent!

SIRSHREE: People who devised these traditions had a certain objective in mind – that we should do something that can help the departed person's journey ahead.

The fact is that there is only one thing we can do to help them in their journey, and that is to use the power of thoughts in the form of our prayers. This can help them in Part Two. It is only prayers that can help everywhere, be it on this Earth or in the whole universe, either with the gross body or the subtle body. Therefore, it is crucial to pray.

For this reason, certain days are fixed to offer some prayers for the deceased so that you do not forget to pray for them. People cannot pray without the aid of rites and rituals. The mind being unstable, keeps running wild and cannot focus on prayer. Hence, certain rituals are devised to help the mind to focus on prayer. Some arrangements are made, certain objects of worship are used, so that the feeling and atmosphere for prayer is created. People have woven a lot of rituals around these prayers to help the mind concentrate.

While teaching, a teacher devises the lessons keeping in mind the student who is weakest in studies. If these lessons improve the concentration of the weakest student, it means that they will improve the concentration of everyone. Similarly, the rites and rituals are designed keeping in mind the people who have low concentration and con-sciousness levels.

People also have the fear that if they do not do all this for *their* ancestors, their future genera-tions will not perform these rituals for *them*, and they will then have to face difficulties in the next world. Because of this fear, they ask their children also to be a part of what they are doing for their ancestors so that they should not forget or lose the habit of these ceremonies. They fear that if the children forget, what would happen for their salvation? This cycle goes on. However, their fears are unfounded.

If you have acquired the knowledge of the truth, there is no need to fear anything. Ask yourself why you are performing all these ceremonies. Carry them out only if you are doing them out of feelings of love and affection for the departed. On the other hand, you do not have to wait for a ceremony to pray for them. Prayer can be offered anytime.

Sam: Does this mean we should pray for the dead?

Sɪʀsʜʀᴇᴇ: Certainly. But also ask yourself whether the deceased really needs the prayers you are offering. If that person has lived a dishonest and bad life on Earth, then definitely pray for him. If he has lived a troubled life and has troubled others during his lifetime, then he surely needs your prayers. But if he has lived a peaceful, happy and good life, then he does not need your prayers. In fact, there are some people in Part Two who pray for people in Part One.

Even today, science knows very little about the power of prayer. People are not much aware about the miracles that prayers can bring about. If all the people across the globe pray together at the same time just for two minutes, a world war could be averted. A two-minute collective prayer can do unimaginable wonders. A single collective prayer can end all the miseries of this world. Therefore, pray together for the person who has left his gross body.

There is an exceedingly powerful force generated when a group of people get together and pray for a particular objective. Their combined good thoughts and feelings can eliminate the ignorance, the hatred, the confusion and ego from the mind of the departed.

Group prayers are extremely powerful. They contain strong vibrations of collective strength, power, relation and intention. These vibrations keep on growing and increasing until they permeate the entire universe with those feelings. In such an environment, negative feelings such as discrimination, wrongful desires and atheism get completely uprooted and get replaced by positive feelings such as universal brotherhood, love, oneness and supreme faith. The tradition of group prayers for the departed is, therefore, prevalent in almost all religions. To pray with others and for others purifies the mind.

You need to rid yourself of your false notions and beliefs. If, after getting liberated from your beliefs, you have to perform any rituals because of pressure from your family or relatives, you can do it. But you should be very clear from within as to why you are doing them. If there are no such restrictions imposed by your family, you can easily discard the rites and rituals without any fear.

Certain rituals are performed as protective or precautionary measures. The idea is fine so far. But what follows – certain rites to be carried out after eleven months or in a particular sacred city – is not correct. Some so-called holy men have vested interests in keeping such traditions alive. Some priests even ask if you want to perform the ritual costing Rs. 50 or Rs. 500. Their reasoning is that the one costing Rs. 500 will speed up the process of acquiring nirvana. They say that the one costing Rs. 50 will also do the job, but will take more time. Those who had originally devised the rites and rituals had done so with a lot of care and understanding. The real meaning, however, is lost with the passage of time. Now, just the traditions have remained while the understanding behind them has disappeared. People are performing rituals only out of superstitions and not out of understanding.

Sam: I understand that you recommend group prayers. Is that why mourning meetings were devised?

SIRSHREE: Yes, group prayers are powerful. And the significance of mourning meetings was the same. But, with time, the meaning was lost.

Say, someone has passed away. People have come together to mourn his loss. But individually, everyone is preoccupied thinking about his own affairs.

There is then no use of arranging such a meeting. A mourning or a condolence meet will achieve its purpose only when everyone stops thinking about everything else and actually pray collectively for the departed. As mentioned before, praying in a group has very powerful effects. The purpose of the meeting is that everyone who was touched by the life of the departed can come together at one place and pray for him at the same time. If that is not happening, if people have gathered just to make themselves seen at the meeting or due to fear of other people criticising them for not holding on to tradition, then there is no use of such a meeting.

Sam: My uncle had given a lot of financial help to my father. My father always used to say that we owe him a lot for where we are today. That is the only thing that makes me sorrowful. I don't know anything else about him. I feel detached. What should I say so that my gratitude reaches him?

SIRSHREE: If someone has done something good for you, then you can offer thanksgiving or a gratitude prayer for him. The feeling with which you are offering prayers is more important than the words. You can use any kind of words in your prayer, but they should be filled with deep feeling. If you remember the deceased, recalling the good deeds he had done, that too is a form of prayer. It is not true that prayer is offered only through the medium of words. If you shed tears for him, feel thankful to him and say a few words about him, that too is a prayer. Whatever good he has done, if it is repeated in words, that is also a kind of prayer.

Actually, if you feel thankful to a person, you should let him know about your feelings, especially while he is alive. People tend to express their gratitude only after the death of a person.

When a person retires from a company, where he has worked for a long time, people praise him a lot. They wax eloquent about his work, his team spirit, and his contribution to the company. His colleagues tend to outdo each other in finding adjectives to applaud him. At that time, the person who is retiring thinks, 'If they had told me these things earlier, I would have worked much better. Now that I am leaving, everybody is saying such good things about me'. It is, therefore, very important to show your gratitude and love when a person is alive.

Thus, thank people around you here in Part One and offer thanksgiving prayers for those who have departed to Part Two.

A simple thank you is not just a feeling, but a heartfelt emotion from deep within. You do not have to use bombastic language to offer this prayer or express your gratitude. You do not have to chant special mantras or religious hymns to pray. The words coming from deep within your heart are the best prayers.

Sam: I shall always remember that. As you know, I do have questions on heaven and hell as well as reincarnation. I shall ask them next Wednesday. But one specific question about my uncle. When I received the call yesterday, it was from the army informing me of his helicopter crash. The person who called me tried to console me and said that God had chosen my uncle and called him, he had now become a resident of heaven, and so on. I felt amused and wondered what Sirshree would say about why people usually use such words related to death.

SIRSHREE: These things are said to avoid confusion among the relatives. If people are told the truth, they will be puzzled. If they are told that the physical body of the person has perished, but the subtle body is still continuing the journey, they will be bewildered. When someone dies, all kinds of people are present there, including children. Everyone cannot understand these facts; and also under those circumstances not all are prepared to listen to the real answer. If in that kind of environment, someone tells them, 'He has not actually died,' there is a possibility that the situation would become more complicated.

Actually, every individual realises two follies after his own death. The first is that he was not the physical body. This is because he can see his physical body separate from him after his death. The other folly that he discovers is that he is not

91

'dead'. What he was considering as death is not death at all.

If after the death of a person someone says, 'Oh! He has come to know about two of his follies,' people will not understand and may wonder what he was talking about. It would be baffling for them. To avoid confusion and to lessen their grief, it is said that God has chosen him to stay with Him in heaven, and so on.

When someone dies, we feel sorrow and pity for him and we wonder what will happen to him. What would the poor soul be in his next birth – human, dog, horse, what? For finding this out, certain rituals are performed. People also think about which world he might have reached. Pundits and priests are consulted. The pundits and priests don't know a thing. They give the same answers that their predecessors have handed down to them over generations. So, people get readymade answers. The priests teach the same to their sons, and their business continues uninterrupted.

Some expressions are generally used to soothe the nerves of people whose near and dear one has departed, such as, 'He has gone in the shelter of God', 'God has chosen him and called him', 'He is now residing in heaven and is happy there'. These things are told to make them feel good. They want a reassurance that their near and dear one has a good life after death. Therefore, it is customary to say such things. Only good things are said about the deceased, so as to avoid hurting anybody's feelings. Anything negative uttered may upset the already distressed relatives.

Sam: About this whole thing on heaven and hell and rebirth, I do have a few questions. I shall ask them on Wednesday. Thank you today for your time, Sirshree. I go from here with a very clear mind.

Sɪʀsʜʀᴇᴇ: Be clear in your head and stabilised in the heart. And remember to contemplate on the question Sirshree asked you. Use the funeral this evening as an opportunity to contemplate. The Buddha used to recommend that his monks meditate inside burial grounds. Ramana Maharshi contemplated on death and attained stabilisation. Contemplation on death is a beautiful meditation. Meditate on death and eradicate your follies. This is my blessing for you today. Thank you for the opportunity of serving you.

WEEK SEVEN

Residing in Heaven and Returning to Earth?

Sameer performed the last rites of his uncle on Sunday evening. He asked his family members to close their eyes and offer a special prayer for him. The event was over without any hiccups, and relieved, Sameer returned home.

On Monday, Sameer received an invitation for his friend's engagement party at the Taj Hotel. He enjoyed visiting such places as he loved to eat good food. He considered himself a connoisseur of world cuisine. He wrapped up his work for the day and drove to the hotel. He congratulated his friend and his fiancée and was soon surveying the mouth watering buffet. He took a plate for himself and took such huge helpings of all that was lined up, that the food on his plate looked like a pyramid.

He found a table at a corner and within twenty minutes everything vanished and his plate was neat and clean. He was getting ready for another helping when it dawned on him how much his palate controlled him. Without a second thought, he dumped his plate, said his goodbyes and drove back home.

It was Tuesday. He began noticing how self aware he was of his actions. He had started to see everything in Part One in a different way and started questioning how it would be in Part Two. He felt a strange stillness within. Nothing happened without his consent. It was as if his mind was obeying everything that he was saying. 'This is it', he thought. 'Nothing can disturb this newly found peace. A tamed mind is like a still pond without ripples. But how long will this state last? How would Part Two be? Would there be television in Part Two? Presumably not.' He reached his office, but his contemplation continued throughout the day.

After work, he came home and watched a documentary on his DVD player titled 'The Tibetan Book of the Dead'. He also began to share what he had learnt with others, especially his near and dear ones. He was eager to meet Sirshree, as the question of rebirth constantly tugged at his mind. Wednesday came and Sameer finally felt like he was going to be reborn.

Sam: Sirshree, it's funny that I should say this, but I had a great funeral!

Sirshree: Yes, if understood correctly, death is a celebration. A dead body also teaches us a lot of things. When a person dies, he can become instrumental for others to learn some things. If, at such times, people contemplate deeply over death, they can make their lives better. Otherwise, in their busy lives, they don't get that time for contemplation. So, what did you do?

Sam: Since my uncle was a Hindu, I had his body cremated. I decided that I should use that method which his gross body would have observed the most in its lifetime here, so that his subtle body gets the signal that it should continue its journey in case it was still attached to its life here. I chose the quickest possible way to cremate him and did not perform any ritual whatsoever. Plus, I do not intend to do anything in the coming days. I did only one thing – I asked all my relatives to close their eyes and pray for him.

SIRSHREE: What did you ask them to pray for?

Sam: That his journey beyond should begin as soon as possible and progress smoothly. Also he should get the right guidance there and he should be receptive for it.

SIRSHREE: That's good, Sameer! Just as you are a volunteer here in Tej Gyan Foundation, there are volunteers there who can help him.

Sam: I noticed some interesting things in the crematorium. There were a couple of other funerals going on. In one of the funerals, a young man, presumably the son, was performing the rites with his head shaved. I thought that the reason they must have introduced the custom of shaving the head in India was so that it serves as an indication to everyone that someone has died in the family, so that they will behave appropriately. I am also happy that nowadays in India, people have moved beyond this tradition and very rarely does someone shave his head. At least, not in the cities.

SIRSHREE: The other reason why this ritual was introduced is to make the son feel responsible for the family, now that his father has passed away. His shaved head reminds him of his responsibility.

Sam: Interesting! Some elders attending my uncle's funeral insisted on taking a bath at the crematorium before returning to their homes. I presume this ritual must have been introduced from the point of view of cleanliness.

SIRSHREE: Yes. Another reason for introducing this ritual was that taking a bath signifies that now there is no relationship left with that dead person. In this way, thoughts of fear are also washed away.

Sam: I once again want to thank you for your guidance. I feel very liberated.

SIRSHREE: And have you contemplated on what Sirshree asked you?

Sam: Yes. Sirshree had asked me to contemplate on the significance of knowing about life after death. Additionally, I was supposed to reflect on why Sirshree had brought up the topic of death in response to my initial question about feeling a vacuum in my life.

SIRSHREE: Yes.

Sam: I have understood that the state of mind now has a bearing on the state of mind later. And based on the state of mind and thereby level of conscious-

97

ness, where and with whom I stay in Part Two gets determined. Hence, it is important to train the mind in this life. I have begun noticing how my craving for chocolates and sweets is a dangerous habit, not only in Part One, but in Part Two also. The whole process is beautiful. I did not have to force myself. But, with understanding, I am beginning to notice and get rid of my cravings.

SIRSHREE: Now let's assume that you let your cravings go unchecked. You don't train your mind. And soon the cravings become an addiction. What happens then? Those who live on the lower sub-planes in the other world continue to engage in satisfying their cravings for food – not the food we have on Earth, the food there is different – and drinks and sleep. They cannot forget their physical craving for food and drinks so easily. Therefore, they eat and drink just out of habit rather than necessity. Food is not required to nourish the body in the subtle world. Yet, they continue to think about food and create food.

At the higher levels, people do not crave physical gratification; they don't feel the necessity for all such things. There, as a person progresses and brings purity in his thoughts, he adds radiance and beauty to his persona.

Sam: I have also begun to understand that if I want to gain entry to the higher sub-planes of consciousness, I have to train myself in this life for spiritual growth there.

SIRSHREE: No, spiritual growth and attaining the fifth is possible with any body – gross or subtle. So, why not begin now? Continue to practise what you have learnt in the retreats here to access and attain the Self. The Self experiences Itself when the mind drops. For growth in Part Two, train your mind in Part One itself. Train your mind to defocus. Train your mind to be devoid of cravings.

Spiritual growth is the focus *now*. Not later. If you attain the truth in your life here, your future life will be beautiful. Your happiness will increase manifold. If you do not attain the truth in your life here, then in Part Two you will realise your mistake as well as the wasted opportunity and time. When the film of your entire life is replayed in front of your eyes during the grey period, you will lament, 'Alas! I had the opportunity of acquiring the Supreme Knowledge when it came knocking at my door and I did not take it'. Therefore, know the true purpose of life. Understand it and work towards it.

Sam: So, what is the key training the mind needs in this life to be prepared for the next?

SIRSHREE: The mind has to be made unwavering, pure, loving. You have come to this Earth with a mind. Make it an unwavering mind, a pure mind, a steadfast mind, a loving mind. And attain the knowledge of the Self, of the truth.

Going ahead from here, in your long journey in the next world, it is the knowledge of truth that will be of supreme value, not money. In the other world, you cannot reach a higher level by bribing anyone. Money simply does not come into the picture. So many troubles on this Earth are because man has to fill his stomach and cure diseases of his physical body. All these things require money. In the other world, there are no such hassles of the physical body such as food, disease or money. You should get inspired by these facts. You should learn your lessons faster on this Earth and increase your level of understanding as soon as possible. You should try to attain the highest levels of consciousness in this life, so that in the other world too you can reach the higher pedestals of self-expression.

You have read and understood about some beliefs and some secrets about life after death. If, from this knowledge, you can learn to utilise your time on Earth to the fullest to attain understanding, then there is some use of acquiring such knowledge. Otherwise, it is in vain.

Sam: Yes, Sirshree. I now realise this. I am still slightly confused. But for the most part, the picture is clear.

SIRSHREE: At this point you do not have the complete picture of life and death. Therefore, you are confused. But when you see the complete picture, you will realise that the entire picture is full of joy – there is joy in the beginning, joy in the middle, and at the end. The only thing there is – joy. What is it that you are still unclear about? You mentioned some questions last Wednesday.

Sam: Yes, Sirshree. I have some questions on heaven, hell, rebirth and ghosts. My first question is whether the higher levels of consciousness in Part Two are generally referred to as 'heaven' and lower levels as 'hell'?

SIRSHREE: Are you clear that heaven and hell are not ready-made places that exist in the skies where people are sent after their death?

Sam: Yes, Sirshree.

SIRSHREE: Actually, a person creates his own heaven or hell in Part Two, through the feelings and thoughts he harbours. If he has positive feelings and thoughts, he creates an environment which can be regarded as 'heaven'. If he has negative feelings and thoughts such as hatred and jealousy, he will create an environment which can be regarded as 'hell'. That hell is not like the hell as depicted in popular folklore, but a place where a person of higher consciousness is not comfortable. Only a person of lower levels of consciousness can live in those surroundings. And he continues to stay there until his negative thoughts turn into positive and happy thoughts.

He who is living in hell does not realise that he is living in hell. There is heaven and hell on this Earth too. When you see people suffering due to their wrong notions and beliefs, what do you think about them? You look at their misery and feel, 'They are still stuck in such wretched beliefs; they are living in hell!' But when you point this out to them, they will rebuke you. You can see their hell but they cannot see it. You have become free of your limiting beliefs. How happy you feel! You find yourself living in heaven. Hence, you tell them that they are still living in hell. They, however, refuse to believe you.

Similarly, in the other world, when the subtle bodies whose level of consciousness is high see people at lower levels, they will say, 'How unfortunate! You are still bound by your false beliefs and misconceptions. If you had got rid of them on Earth, you would not have to live in the miserable condition you are living now.' However, people at lower levels are not ready to listen or believe that they are living in hell. The irony is that they have created hell with their own thoughts without realising it is hell. Therefore, they do not even think about getting rid of it by creating something new – *which they can*. Hence, due to their ignorance, they continue to live in hell!

Like there are people of lower consciousness living on Earth, so also there are subtle bodies with lower consciousness living in the other world, but at their own sub-planes or environments. People of higher levels can see people of lower levels of consciousness living in hell. The one who is at a higher level can recognise the lower levels. However, those who are at the lower levels can never recognise the higher levels.

Higher levels can be achieved only through spiritual practice or *sadhana*, meditation, contemplation and understanding. If you have to understand the Supreme, you have to become the Supreme. Mediocrity can be understood very easily. Just by looking at a person you can make out what beliefs he is living with. You can also understand the thoughts that must be arising within him due to those beliefs, and the misery and pain he must be going through due to those thoughts. Beliefs can only produce greed about heaven and fear about hell, which will in turn lead to sorrow. If you have reached the higher levels, you can easily see the hell, which people cannot see despite living there.

Sam: Ah, very beautiful! But, Sirshree, why were the concepts of heaven and hell created?

SIRSHREE: The concept of hell was created in order to produce fear in the minds of people here on Earth, so as to make them follow the righteous path. Likewise, they are given enticement in terms of heaven to compel them to perform good deeds. All the ideas of heaven and hell are wrong. People who spread such fears of hell and give false promises of heaven are also living with false beliefs. You have to realise today that this knowledge about death and life after death should only help you to understand one thing – to use this life on Earth for increasing your level of understanding. If knowledge about heaven and hell helps you in further enhancing your level of understanding, it is fine. Otherwise, there is no use of such knowledge.

When you reach the highest levels of consciousness in that world, you will understand these things by default. You do not need to understand them today. However, if this knowledge enhances your thinking today, if it helps you realise the importance of your spiritual practice today, then it is of use to you.

Sam: My other question was regarding rebirth. Hinduism and Buddhism say it exists. Christianity and Islam say it does not exist. Sirshree has only talked about going to Part Two. How about returning to Part One?

SIRSHREE: Could it be possible that both are right – both Hinduism and Buddhism on one hand and Christianity and Islam on the other?

Sam: How, Sirshree?

SIRSHREE: Do you remember Sirshree talked about memories being used?

Sam: Yes, when I had read a quote on people being brought to Earth from Part Two to help humanity. But I did not understand it.

SIRSHREE: The journey of the subtle body continues for thousands of years. One way of putting it is that if the lifespan here is taken as a hundred years, the lifespan in Part Two is of the order of ten thousand years.

Sam: I understand there is no notion of time in Part Two and that you are only giving a relative idea.

SIRSHREE: Yes. And after the lifespan of the subtle body, the subtle body ends. That should be termed as 'death'. It has been expressed as 'the fifth' or 'the Self merging into the Self'. Thus, the limited human consciousness finally gets liberated and merges into the unlimited Oneness, into God. You can express it as 'nothing' or 'everything'. So you can call all of this one birth – the journey from the gross body to the subtle body. However, at the end of the lifespan of the subtle body, the memories could be used. Memories of one body can be used in another body. A combination of memories could be used. And people misinterpret that as reincarnation.

Sam: There are examples of people remembering their past lives. Is that because memories are used?

SIRSHREE: Yes. Say, you are constructing a building. The body and mind are akin to the 'material' used in construction. You then dismantle and use some part of the material in another building. You can either call that as the same building or another building having the same materials.

Sam: So, I am born again in a sense?

SIRSHREE: In what sense is the key question. If you are talking about 'Sameer', the individual, the one who considers himself to be the body, then he is not reborn. Sameer is attached to the gross body as an individual. If Sameer is not stabilised, then Sameer shall continue to be attached to the subtle body while considering himself to be an individual. All his tendencies shall be carried forward. When the subtle body ends, the individual also ends. So from the point of view of the individual – the ego – there is no rebirth. Now – it is possible that the memories in that body may be used by the Self in another body.

Sam: Thus, from the point of Self, there is rebirth. The Self is reborn?

Sɪʀsʜʀᴇᴇ: The Self was never born. Hence, it can never die. So even from that perspective, there is no rebirth.

Sam: You were saying that it is possible that memories may be used. Is it possible that memories may not be used?

Sɪʀsʜʀᴇᴇ: Yes.

Sam: I am feeling bad. I thought there would be some continuity. It pains me to hear that there is an end.

Sɪʀsʜʀᴇᴇ: It pains the individual. You are the Self. Your true nature is that of the fifth – Pure Consciousness. For the 'real you', it does not make a difference. If there is some pain on hearing this, then some more understanding has to be gained.

Let us talk about two sentences. The first one is: 'Death is the ultimate reality; everything else is a

myth. Everyone is going to die one day.' Anyone
who hears this will say, 'There is so much logic in
this, this is indeed the truth. Death is the ultimate
truth, as everyone dies one day.' Then you hear
someone say, 'Death is an illusion'. When you hear
such statements that are totally opposite to each
other, you get bewildered. You oscillate between
the two as you don't know what to believe. The
mind says that it would have been better if you
were presented with only one aspect. However,
from different points of view, both the aspects are
correct.

Sam: Once again, Sirshree, how?

SIRSHREE: If you can take a holistic view of both the dimensions, you will clearly understand the truth behind
the two apparently contradictory statements. The
first statement says death is the ultimate truth. This
is said taking the external body into consideration.
Fearing the death of his body, man dies a thousand times before his actual death. Therefore, he
is told that death will one day embrace everyone,
so there is no point in fearing death.

The other statement is from the point of view
of 'Consciousness' or 'Self'. It talks about the Self
which is distinct from the body-mind mechanism.
Death as the ultimate truth is meant for the
gross body. On the other hand, for the 'Self' or
'Consciousness' that is within all of us, it is said,
'You cannot die. Death is an illusion. Therefore,
die whilst you are alive, that is, kill the ego.'

[Ego here refers to the feeling of apparent separateness from the rest of creation].

On one hand, it is said, 'Don't die a little death every day out of fear'. On the other, it is said, 'Die as soon as possible'. Through this, you will understand that knowledge is imparted not just to the individual or body-mind, but also to the consciousness that is within you. When you understand this, you will understand both the statements.

When you take a bird's eye view – a helicopter view or a holistic approach – after listening to both statements you will agree to both viewpoints. You have to understand what is being said to whom. Who is being told that you are not going to have a rebirth? Whose rebirth is going to take place? Those who have understood the essence of God try to express God in different words and from different viewpoints.

Only when you attain the whole truth and take a helicopter view, will all four dimensions be visible to you at the same time. And then the entire picture will be clear in front of you. Not before that.

Sam: Wonderful, Sirshree! Apparent contradictions on rebirth now seem clear.

Sirshree: Rebirth can be understood only when you know who is the one being born. Understand this with an example and contemplate over it as much as you can.

There is a person by the name of Rama. Rama

works in a drama company. Rama sometimes enacts the role of Shakuntala and sometimes the role of Shakuni. Will you say that Shakuntala has taken rebirth as Shakuni in her next life? If you want to call this rebirth, you can. You should understand that the same fundamental principle, the Consciousness, is playing the roles of different characters. Externally, it appears that everyone is reborn. This happens because every character uses imprinted memories. This has led to the false belief that an individual is born. The individual or the ego is just a rumour – how can it be born?

Sam: Then, is the concept in Hinduism that you are born again on this Earth wrong? Is the concept of Judgement Day in Islam or Christianity wrong?

Sɪʀsʜʀᴇᴇ: What do you understand about Judgement Day?

Sam: Well, what I have heard about Judgement Day is that when a person dies, he rests in his grave. Then there will be the Judgement Day when God will wake the dead up from their graves. If they have lived their lives the right way according to the holy book, if they have followed the word of the Prophet, then they will be granted life again. They will be granted such a life in which there will be no death.

Sɪʀsʜʀᴇᴇ: There are various aspects to life after death. One aspect is that of the journey of the subtle body beyond the gross body. Another aspect is that of the subtle body also ending and Consciousness merging into the Self which can be referred to as 'death'. The third aspect is that of living on this Earth and preparing for Part Two. The fourth aspect is of evolution to higher planes of consciousness in Part Two.

You know that before starting any venture, you have to prepare your mind for that task. The truth seems to be illogical in this illusory physical world. Upon hearing anything illogical or para-doxical, the mind says, 'I don't agree with this. I am not going to start this work. I do not wish to live my life as per these religious doctrines and holy books'. Therefore, people are presented with only a part of the truth so as to get them to agree to follow the path of truth. This is done so that people can live a life of righteousness and virtue. Leading their lives this way, and meditating and contemplating on the truth, they will realise the whole truth one day.

Those who have penned down their experience of Self in religious texts, be it the Bible, the Koran, the Guru Granth Sahib or the Vedas, did they not know the complete truth? They were all aware of the complete truth, but they also knew the whole truth may be difficult to understand as it seems illogical. Therefore, according to the level of un-derstanding or eligibility of the people in front of them, they presented only a part of the truth. Say, if out of four, you are presented with only two aspects of a particular entity, you would definitely get baffled. Similarly, you can take it that on the subject of rebirth, you have been presented with only two out of four aspects of the truth, which has led to all the confusion.

Sam: Thus, the concept of being born again as animals on Earth in Hinduism or Buddhism or the concept of Judgement Day in Christianity or Islam was only propounded to make people live a better life here?

Sirshree: If the figure '6' is written on the floor, people looking at it from the other side would read it as '9'. People on this side would, however, read it as '6' only. Though it is one and the same number, yet there is such a marked difference in the way it is understood. The one who wrote it knew what he was writing, but people reading it will look at it from different perspectives.

If people cannot understand the two facets of a particular entity, how will they cope if four aspects are to be presented to them? There will be complete chaos. Therefore, every religion has presented only one aspect, as people may not be able to understand multiple facets of a particular entity.

Only one aspect is revealed, so that people understand it and start living good and moral lives. If they are confused with a number of aspects, they will never be able to make a beginning. The subject of rebirth has four dimensions. Only two have been told till today and people are confused.

Sam: People are confused and I am clear (*smiles*). Sirshree, I have been meaning to ask you something for the last two to three meetings. My wife lost her brother six years ago in an accident. Ever since then, she becomes sad whenever she remembers him. Can I bring her to the next meeting so that you can counsel her?

SIRSHREE: She is welcome. Tell her what you have heard here. There is a need of a book on this topic so that anybody who needs help can read it and get clear. And then they could come here if they have any more questions. But for now, tell her what you know. Show her the pictures you had drawn to represent the bodies.

Sam: I have been making notes of what Sirshree has been saying. I will refer to them and try to represent you adequately. Maybe, these notes can be used as material for a book.

SIRSHREE: Yes, Sameer. But first, you become clear. There are many more aspects that you have to understand regarding how the mind is to be trained on life on Earth, so as to prepare for Part Two. Contemplate on that. That's all for today. Thank you for the opportunity of serving you.

Sorrow and Suicide

Sameer had a much clearer picture now. He spent his week thinking on how he could make his life better here so he could be prepared for Part Two. He also told his wife that she could meet Sirshree and receive counselling on her grief over her brother's death. Mona was thrilled at hearing this. Her brother had died suddenly in a road accident six years earlier. He was twenty-five years when he died and Mona, twenty years. It was as if the world had collapsed for her. She could still remember the three years of depression and grief she went through – waking up in the middle of the night and screaming; clinging to any object of her brother; crying all night.

Three years back, when her friend asked her to meet Sirshree, Mona agreed. Sirshree listened to Mona patiently for thirty minutes in their first meeting and when she had finished, had asked Mona to do a very simple thing which had benefited her immensely. 'Mona, look at yourself. You are sitting crouched and your fists are clenched. If you want to come out of your depression, just do one thing for a week. Whenever you notice that your body is taut, open up. Practise for a week having an open body language. Whenever you see your fists are clenched, open them. Meet Sirshree in a week.' Mona met Sirshree a week later and told him that she felt much better. Sirshree then told her to pray every day for her brother and also taught her the art of acceptance and invited her to attend his retreats.

That was three years back. She had subsequently met and married Sameer and together with him, was progressing on the spiritual path under Sirshree's guidance. Though her depression had vanished, her grief had not. Whenever there was an incident that reminded her of her brother, tears filled her eyes. Sirshree had said that with the understanding of life, the grief would also pass. When Sameer started talking about Sirshree's teachings of Life after Death, Mona thought she was finally comprehending something about what life was. She had found many answers in what Sameer revealed to her. But that had given rise to many questions too. The death of Sameer's uncle had also brought many painful memories back. She eagerly looked forward to meeting Sirshree again, and have her questions clarified.

SIRSHREE: Mona, Sirshree has been reading your letters where you have reported your spiritual progress. Sirshree is pleased that you are very happy.

Mona: Yes, Sirshree. After the Sadhana Retreat, not only did I understand how the mind behaves, I could transcend the mind too. I have not experienced as much happiness and bliss in my whole life that I experienced in the last two years. I cannot ask anything more from life. But, a part of me died with my brother. I still feel bereaved, though it no longer troubles me.

SIRSHREE: So, you have grief. But you are not grieving over grief.

Sam: Yes, Sirshree. I don't think Mona grieves at all. And you said it very beautifully. With sadhana, she has come to terms with her grief.

Mona: But the grief does not go away.

Sɪʀsʜʀᴇᴇ: What had Sameer told you about our recent conversations?

Mona: Everything. He is very meticulous. He notes down everything and tells me. And thanks for giving him a whack over logic (*smiles*).

Sɪʀsʜʀᴇᴇ: And has what Sameer told you made a difference?

Mona: Yes. Because I now realise that my brother has not 'gone away'. His subtle body still continues. It has helped reduce the grief. But when Sameer's uncle passed away over the weekend, it all came back – especially when I saw his dead body.

Sam: Sirshree has given a very good analogy to help overcome such grief. When a person's near and dear ones die, he feels very sad. He is asked why he is sad. Say, a relative of yours goes to the United States to get treated for a disease. He recovers after the treatment. But the doctors have advised him to stay there as that environment is good for his health. So, will you feel sad? You will say, 'Why should we feel sad? Our relative is in the US; he is recovering well. What else do we want?' You do not cry for a relative who has gone away for treatment and has decided to stay there. A similar thing has happened when a close one has passed away. You think that something bad has happened with him. But it is not so. If that relative could speak to you, he would have told you, 'If you really want to help me, then stop crying. Please do not cry for me, at least. You may cry for yourself, but not for me'.

Mona: Yes. I have understood this part about my brother still being there as well as being fine in Part Two. But what is the meaning of 'crying for myself', not crying for him?

SIRSHREE: OK, let us take an example to understand this.

A man was crying at a rich person's grave. Someone asked him, 'Was that rich man a relative of yours?' He said no. That person was puzzled and asked him again, 'If he was not your relative, then why are you crying for him?' He replied, 'That's the reason I am crying. Alas! If he had been my relative, he would have left a lot of wealth and property for me'. This shows that he was crying not for the rich man, but at his own misfortune.

Ask yourself, are you crying because you miss him? Or because you think it is unfair that he passed away at a young age?

Mona: Both.

SIRSHREE: If you are crying for yourself, it is fine. But do not cry for him thinking that it's unfortunate for him that he is not in this world anymore. Those who die are very happy in their journey in the next world. They are interested in the journey ahead.

They do not want to take a step backwards because their onward journey is important for them. If you really want to do something for someone who has died, you can do two things – first, do not cry; second, pray for him.

Pray for those who have departed, because prayers have immense power. Thoughts have the greatest impact in the journey of the subtle body. Therefore, have pure and positive thoughts for the deceased. Pray for the success of their journey ahead. Pray that they come out of their old beliefs and notions as soon as possible. Pray for them that they receive the right guidance in their life in Part Two.

Mona: I remember, Sirshree, you had asked me to pray for my brother. I did it every day for a year. I always thought you asked me to pray because that was a way for me to overcome my depression.

SIRSHREE: Yes. And for one more reason. Understand very clearly what happens when you grieve. This is important, Mona. The subtle body could be still attached and interested in its relatives here. If your brother would have seen you crying and grieving inconsolably for many days, he would have felt sad. The moment he feels sad, he has begun creating pictures of sadness and depression around him. And in Part Two, everything is a game of thoughts. He can get entangled in those thoughts.

Mona: Oh! So, my thoughts would have caused him trouble!

SIRSHREE: Whenever you grieve, it is like tapping someone on his shoulder from behind when that person is on a journey. It is better to pray. And Mona, it is your prayer for him that shall affect him more. For instance, Sameer's prayers for him are not as important as your prayers, since he is more interested in you.

Mona: Oh!

SIRSHREE: There is another reason why you should pray. People are born in different hospitals on this Earth. Some hospitals have expert doctors, so the children born there have a very smooth entry into the world. Likewise, we should pray for our relatives that they enter Part Two under the guidance of experts so that they can continue smoothly on their journey with the subtle body. If they have done some wrong deeds in their physical life, you should definitely pray that they enter the other world through a particularly good hospital and meet good people to guide them. Just like all facilities are given to a baby as soon as it is born here, similarly, guides and mentors are immediately made available to you on your entry there. But who will you listen to?

For example, you have gone to visit a new place, and four people appear before you with guide maps. Whom will you listen to? You encounter one guide and then another and so forth. You have a number of guides in front of you. What do you do? You have to choose. Some guides tell you what you like to hear and you choose that guide. You will, therefore, choose a guide depending on your level of understanding. Hence, pray that he gets the best guide and that he is open to advice and guidance. These prayers are best done immediately after death.

Mona: Sirshree, will I meet my brother when my gross body dies?

SIRSHREE: You could. A person who has died can meet his relatives in the subtle world who have died before him, if he wants to. The reason is that the scale of time on Earth is different from that of the subtle world.

Mona: How long does the subtle body live, Sirshree?

Sam: Sirshree had said about ten thousand years.

SIRSHREE: That was just an example. One hundred years on this Earth can be said to be equivalent to one year of the subtle world. These words are being used to explain something which cannot be explained in the language we use on Earth because the dimensions and criteria of that world are totally different. But we will have to use this language for the sake of explanation. Do not take it too literally.

Sam: But would ten thousand years be an incorrect answer?

SIRSHREE: The answer to this question is that the life of the physical body can be measured in days, months and years, which is not so with the subtle body.

We have a day consisting of twenty-four hours for the proper functioning of this physical body. Time here is determined on the basis of the moon, sun and stars in relation to Earth.

On this Earth, it takes a lot of time to travel from one place to another as there is the limitation of the physical body. If you did not have your physical body, you could have reached any place easily, within seconds. The concept of time is born due to the limitation of the physical body.

Science is trying to find out what the states of timelessness and spacelessness are like. It is being predicted that within a certain period of time, people will know about newer dimensions. Due to the speed at which science is progressing today, very soon there will be a time when a layman will be able to understand all these aspects. Science has progressed much more in the last hundred years than it has in the past thousand years. We are, therefore, able to think about such issues today.

In the ages gone by, a scientific language essential for understanding this knowledge did not exist. Hence, this knowledge remained a secret and a mystery for a long time and eventually disappeared. Today, science is developing such machines and chemicals that will help people experience the state of samadhi within the gross body.

The concept of time in the subtle world is totally different from here. We use the language of the Earth in an attempt to explain those concepts by saying that a hundred years on this Earth are equivalent to one year of the subtle world. This is just to give you an idea that the life there is much longer as compared to life here; otherwise it is neither long nor short. This only serves the purpose of comparison.

When you are waiting for someone desperately and that person is not showing up, even a short period of time seems very long. When you keep a thermometer in your mouth to measure your temperature, that one minute seems like eternity. On the other hand, when you are watching an interesting movie, hours seem to fly by. Time is felt more when there is boredom in a gross body. Otherwise, it does not exist at all. It is just a concept.

Just understand that the concept of time is being used here to make you aware that vast time of the gross body is equivalent to a fraction of time of the subtle body.

Mona: I am beginning to understand this a bit. But, Sirshree, I have been wondering why my depression went away when I met you three years back.

SIRSHREE: Because your beliefs changed. You earlier believed that you would never come out of depression.

Mona: So, when you asked me to change my body language, you were breaking my beliefs.

SIRSHREE: There are many ways to break beliefs. This is one of the ways. And now you will stop grieving because your underlying beliefs shall also change. If you had seen since childhood that people celebrate death, they take out a joyful procession on the occasion and make merry, would you then have feared death as you do today? Would you then have cried when your near and dear ones passed away? What would have happened if you had seen celebrations of death since your childhood? Everything is related to beliefs and the way you have been brought up to see those beliefs. Your fears, your sorrows, your joys, your successes, your failures, your life, your death – everything is based on your beliefs.

Beliefs are something that you believe in, but may not actually be true. People have devised beliefs to suit their conveniences, and you react according to them. In fact, you lead your entire life according to them. You have to come out of those beliefs. You need to test whatever you have assumed to be true before incorporating it as your belief. The path of truth says know the reality and then start living a supreme life.

Mona: Sirshree, then why didn't you tell this to me three years back? Why did you not tell me about the journey of the subtle body?

Sirshree: Would you have believed me then? You would have thought Sirshree was telling you things just to help you with your depression. There is a time for everything. At that moment, what was apt for you was told to you. And Mona, when you met

Sirshree at that time, weren't you so depressed that you were contemplating suicide?

Sam: What!

Mona: How did you know, Sirshree?! I never told you this. No one knows. Even Sameer doesn't know.

Sɪʀsʜʀᴇᴇ: You were not ready then for higher knowledge in that state. Your level of consciousness was extremely low. And if the message of life after death has to be revealed, it requires time. Like the ten sessions that Sirshree is spending with Sameer. And you were willing to give that time then. But it was better that you gave that time in understanding some basic lessons of life.

Mona: You are the best judge, Sirshree. I can't thank you enough for what you have done for me. I am so completely out of depression that I can't help wondering who that Mona was.

Sam: Pardon the question, Mona. But, Sirshree, what would have happened if Mona had indeed committed suicide? What would have happened to Mona if she had killed herself?

Sɪʀsʜʀᴇᴇ: Suicide should be termed as killing your own body, not killing your Self. Killing the Self – are you kidding? You cannot kill the Self. The Self is immortal. Therefore, it is emphasised that you should have complete knowledge on this subject. Half-knowledge is very dangerous. Proceeding ahead to Part Two without learning your lessons here in Part One means inviting trouble and enhancing your misery. In the other world, such a person continues to be in escapist tendencies, because his suicide has reinforced the tendency powerfully. He lives a worried life there too, as he has got used to worrying. He is consumed with worries. He just cannot do anything other than worry. Only when you know yourself completely, will you realise that true death is when the subtle body dies. With the death of the subtle body, the role of that body ends, or a choice of a new form of expression begins.

Mona: I do not fully understand. What would have happened if I had committed suicide?

SIRSHREE: The person who ends his own life does not complete his learning on Earth. Due to this, he has the same tendencies in Part Two as he had in Part One. The subtle body has the same habits as that of the gross body since the subtle body is ruled by the same mind. The mental sheath continues to function in the subtle body. His mental sheath is the same – filled with old understanding and tendencies. He will, therefore, try to take his life there too. But he cannot commit suicide again as he no longer has a physical body and the subtle body cannot be killed. As a result, he will be even more miserable in that world. Those who run away from problems once will keep on running away throughout. He has developed the compulsive habit of running away.

A beggar was asking for alms saying that he

was destitute. Someone asked him, 'You seem to be absolutely fine: your hands and legs are okay, you have perfect eyes, nose and ears; why do you call yourself destitute?' He replied, 'I am destitute because of my habit of begging. I have developed the compulsive habit of begging and that's why I am helpless and asking for alms'.

A person who has committed suicide is a slave of his habit of running away from problems.

Mona: Would I have gone to hell? Would I have been at the lower levels of consciousness?

SIRSHREE: Not literal hell. But, if there were a hell, it would be for those who commit suicide. It is hell because when the mind is disturbed, distressed and depressed, then it is actually in hell. Hell is not a physical place but a state of mind. People want to blow their brains out because they are living a hellish life and are very confused. Hell is pictured as a place where one is being roasted in fire but is still not dying, because it is the subtle body and it cannot be annihilated by fire. The person who has the tendency of committing suicide tries to kill his subtle body as well, but it cannot be killed. That is why he is always in turmoil. He wants to run away from that turmoil but is unable to.

Sam: I was narrating what you told me about life after death to a friend. He said, 'If the subtle world is so beautiful, then isn't it logical to end my life now? Why go on with this misery?'

SIRSHREE: Don't even think of making such a blunder. The ones who are most miserable in Part Two are those who have committed suicide. You have come on Earth to learn your lessons. If one puts an end to his body before completing his learning, this implies that he is under a lot of false notions and beliefs. One, who is full of wrong notions and beliefs here, will not be able to live happily in the other world too.

If you cannot understand the true Self in this gross body, how will you know it in the subtle form? If you cannot walk on the ground, how will you walk on a rope? The ultimate goal of man is to know oneself; that is the true Self. The human form has been gifted to you for a specific purpose. Do not lose your precious time. Inculcate patience in this life. Patience will help you even later. Learn all your lessons while being in the gross body. Do not run away from life without completing all your lessons. Every 'body' on Earth is learning his or her lesson. Understand why you should not end your life prematurely so as to experience the subtle world sooner through an example. Tell this example to your friend, Sameer.

Once there was a saint. He went to the forest. He saw a fox whose leg was broken. It could hardly walk. The saint felt sad on seeing this and started wondering how the fox would provide for itself. He saw a lion coming there with its kill. It had its fill and then left the remainder for the fox to feast upon. The saint was overjoyed upon witnessing this incident and exclaimed, 'God has made such a wonderful world! He has made sure that even a lame fox gets food. I was worrying without reason. I will go and sit below the tree and I am sure someone will provide me with food too'. Feeling very happy, he went and sat under a tree. Throughout the day, he kept thinking that he would get food from somewhere. He thought someone would bring him food but no one came. Two days passed and he was still sitting under the tree, hungry. The third day he was almost dying of hunger and called out, 'O God! I trusted you to provide me with food but I did not receive any. You provided for the fox, but not for me'. A voice from the sky answered, 'If you want to copy someone, copy the lion, not the fox'.

You have understood from the fable that it has not been implied in any way that you try to finish this life as soon as possible because you find life in Part Two better. You most definitely have to infer that the more understanding you gain in this world – the greater will be the happiness you will experience in your life in the next world.

You must have seen that it is difficult to convince someone to attend a spiritual discourse or satsang when he is in depression or thinks too highly of himself. He does not readily agree to accompany you. He believes that he does not need it. To get someone who is at a lower level of consciousness to do things of a higher level is very difficult. He considers himself to be in heaven despite being in hell. He, who is in hell at lower levels of consciousness, does not realise that he is in hell. Those who are in heaven at higher levels of consciousness, know that they are in heaven and that the other person with lower consciousness level is in hell. They are aware about themselves as well as others.

If you tell someone that he is living in hell, he will get angry with you. He will say, 'Yes, it is true that there are certain difficulties and problems in my life, but this does not mean that I am in hell. I have seen pictures of hell. It is full of people thrown in scalding oil and roasted over fire'. He will never agree that he is living in hell. Try telling him, 'You are living under the delusion that you are the body. What can you create when you are bound by this limitation? In your life, there is hell today and there shall be hell even later'. He will not accept this. You cannot convince him.

Mona: *(laughs)* I get it. I would have not only gone to hell, I was already in hell when I met you. And thank God, I met you. You convinced me because you showed me experientially how I could lead a life of happy thoughts.

Sam: Yes, Sirshree. Thank you for saving Mona for me.

Sɪʀsʜʀᴇᴇ: If you both do wish to thank Sirshree, then give Sirshree what he asks.

128

Sam: Anything, Sirshree!

Mona: Yes, anything Sirshree wants.

Sirshree: Sirshree wants you to decide what are the 'no-nos' in your life. And promise that it shall remain a no-no. Here, see this sheet that is usually given to college students in Tej Gyan Foundation, a youth programme to help them at an early age.

Go through the table. The first thing mentioned in the table is 'suicide'. Next to it is written 'killing the body'. Not 'killing yourself'. The Self cannot be killed. It is not possible. Mark 'suicide' as 'Never-Never-Never' since you are now aware what happens in reality. Therefore, the table mentions suicide by default. Your consent that it should be on the top of your no-no's list has already been taken. The rest of the table has to be filled by you. Decide what you will never do and what you may do under certain circumstances.

Let us take the example of driving at breakneck speed. Some people are in the habit of driving at high speeds. They should understand that they have no right to harm others because of their bad habit. You may injure yourself by getting into an accident, but you have no right to harm others without any fault of theirs. Driving at high speeds is utterly wrong. You will commit to never driving at high speeds, but in some particular situations where it is really needed, you may drive fast. Make a commitment and mark a tick in the 'No' column.

NO NO'S IN MY LIFE

	Harmful Thoughts and Traits	No	Never
1.	Suicide (Killing of the body)		✓
2.	Negative thinking		
3.	Criticising		
4.	Drugs		
5.	Smoking		
6.	Speed driving	✓	
7.	Alcohol		
8.	Non-vegetarian/Stale food		
9.	Anger		
10.	Backbiting		
11.	Lying		
12.	Bad company		
13.	Sleeping late, waking up late		
14.	Borrowing money		
15.	Wasting money		
16.	Gossiping		
17.	Not keeping things in place		
18.	Others		

Note: Use this table as a guide to matters on which you may need to exercise caution and control.

Mona: I am glad you brought it up. I worry about Sameer's reckless driving. This morning, when we were getting late to reach here, he drove us here in twenty minutes when it usually would have taken forty minutes.

Sam: Sirshree, you always catch the person by his throat (*smiles*). Reckless driving shall be in my list of 'Nos'.

Sɪʀsʜʀᴇᴇ: It need not be a 'never', because there may be emergencies where you may have to drive fast. There are similarly a lot of things that you have to add in the table. This table will be useful for you when you have to make decisions in life. You will never falter in taking a correct and quick decision. You will not have to wait to take advice from someone else. The table will be your guiding star.

Construct this table today and decide on certain principles in your life. The second point in the table is negative thoughts, third is criticism of others, fourth is drugs, the fifth is smoking, and so on. All these habits harm you at the vibrational level and bring down your level of consciousness. The lower the frequency you vibrate at in this life, the higher are the difficulties faced by you in the life after this life.

Those who are balanced and centred easily get rid of their beliefs. Those who are stubborn and rigid have a low frequency, and are stuck with their beliefs. They have to increase the levels of their frequency, knowledge and consciousness.

Mona: You have our word, Sirshree. We shall fill this list and abide by it.

Sam: And it is a small thing Sirshree asked for in return for all that you have done. I was wondering what you would have asked us. In your own unique way, you have got us to commit to something that is for our own benefit.

SIRSHREE: And Mona, can Sirshree ask of you to begin counselling others to overcome depression in life and grief over losing a dear one?

Mona: Definitely, Sirshree. I already feel that with today's added understanding, I need not grieve for my brother. It will only hamper the progress of his journey. And he is fine in his journey. That comforts me. Before our meeting today, I could not have helped others come out of their grief. I have helped others to come out of depression, not grief. Since you have helped me come out of depression, I felt confident about helping others. But, today, I am also confident about helping others overcome the grief of losing a dear one. Thank you, Sirshree.

SIRSHREE: Sameer, you shall be sharing how you are using these teachings to transform your life.

Sam: Yes, Sirshree. Some things have already begun. I shall share the same with you.

SIRSHREE: You can share it next week. But, next time when you come to meet Sirshree, paint a picture of death.

Sam: Meaning?

SIRSHREE: When you come back, tell Sirshree in words or pictures 'What is death?' Most people see death as a monster. They visualise death to be horrible. Now that you have this knowledge, Sirshree would like to see your picture of death or hear your description of all that you have learned here.

Sam: That is a beautiful way of making me contemplate. I shall make an attempt by next Wednesday.

SIRSHREE: Thank you for the opportunity of serving you. And Sameer, drive safely!

The Picture of Death

Mona and Sameer walked out of the meeting room in silence.
It is said: 'When the heart is empty the head doesn't work. But
when the heart is full you don't need the head'.

They hurried out of the building towards the car. Sameer opened
the car and slid behind the wheel. As Mona slid in beside him, he
started the car and rumbled out of the parking. He heard Mona
sobbing and he did not interrupt her. It took them twenty-five minutes
to reach home as Mona's sobbing grew and slowly passed away.
She felt reborn; it was like shedding her old tattered rags and
donning new, pure attire. She felt ten years younger. She wanted
to enjoy the moment and dwell on it without having to speak.

When they reached home, they held hands until Mona recovered
from her reverie. They didn't need words. Both understood that these
were tears of joy at having received crucial guidance at the correct
time. Faith, peace, and gratitude filled their home.

From the next day onwards, Sameer continued to make small
changes in his life. He also contemplated on what the picture of
death would look like. Sirshree's sentence in the last conversation
about being on Earth to learn lessons kept echoing in his mind.

By Tuesday night, he thought he had his picture ready.

Sam: Sirshree, I think I have the picture.

SIRSHREE: Great! Show it.

Sam: I mean it is a verbal picture. I have come up with an analogy that is like a picture.

SIRSHREE: Then describe it.

Sam: Life on Earth is similar to a school. It is a school with a gate that has a lot of beautiful pictures on the outer side, which lures a child to enter. Once the child is in, the gate closes. On the inner side, this gate has a picture of a devil! A child, who has entered through the gate but does not want to go inside the school, turns back and approaches the gate. But the picture of the devil scares the wits out of him. Seeing the picture, the child runs back towards his classroom. The picture of the devil is symbolic of 'death' in our lives. Fearing death, we stay in the school of life and learn the lessons for which we have come here.

Growing up, the child thinks that perhaps there are beautiful things outside and he should venture out, he should put an end to his misery in that school. But once again he sees the picture of the devil on the gate, and quietly continues his further studies in the school. The picture of the devil – fear of death – becomes instrumental in helping him to learn all his lessons well. The child should be able to stay within the school of life before his death arrives otherwise he will get defeated by life and will contemplate ending his own life.

In different classes, at different points of time, teachers teach children various lessons. When the child is young, he is taught easy and simple lessons. More grown up children are taught a level higher and the lessons are more interesting. If someone gets angry easily, he is given a different sort of training. Someone who is jealous and envious of others is given another kind of schooling. Children who are scared are trained to overcome their fears. The lessons of someone who is greedy or one who does not have very good relations with others are unique to him. Each one undergoes customised training depending on his or her needs. Everyone has come to learn his own lessons in this school.

That is my picture. Life is a school in preparation for Part Two very much similar to how education prepares us for our life ahead. The training received in the school continues regardless. The habits learnt in school are seldom easy to break and continue. A child who postpones his studies, postpones his projects at work too. And work life is much longer than school life.

SIRSHREE: Very good, Sameer! The school gate or the fear of death is that limiting line which stops the child from running away from life. Else, countless people would have taken their lives. If we take this example further, other interesting aspects emerge.

The child is studying along with other children in the school. Those children have never seen the world outside either. They consider their school as their entire world. Teachers give children new lessons and the children readily absorb whatever their teachers are telling them. This goes on every single day, day after day.

Sam: Haha! Yes! I am enjoying that you are adding more colours to the picture.

Sirshree: Also, you can say that there is a session in the class wherein the teachers talk about heaven and hell. There is another session in which the topic is destiny and luck. Children lap up these sessions with a lot of interest. With the first session, the children begin their education. In the second session, they make a foundation for future studies. In the third and fourth sessions, they understand some deeper subjects about life. Then they have a recess.

During the recess, children come out of the classroom for the first time. They start playing and strolling in the verandas and playgrounds. There they happen to meet other children from senior classes. When they speak to their seniors, they get puzzled. The senior students tell them that this school of life has a principal too. They were not aware of this. They come to know this only after speaking to their seniors. Children, until then, thought that their class teacher was everything. They did not know that the director of the school was someone else.

Sam: Who is the director of the school? And also, who is the class teacher and what does break or recess time imply?

SIRSHREE: The director of the school is Self, God, Allah, Nature – whatever names you may want to give. The class teacher implies the parents and the teachers, who have maximum influence in the earlier part of our lives. Recess time implies when a person starts encountering bitter as well as sweet experiences in his life. Such circumstances usually appear after a while. From here onwards, a person starts thinking about life from a fresh standpoint. He realises that there is another driving force that governs his life. Till then, he thought that his parents and his teachers comprised his world. Listening to some wise men he comes across in his life, he starts looking at life from a different perspective. By thinking and meditating, he frees himself from the notion of heaven and hell. He is clearer about the concept of destiny and luck. He is now desperate to find the final truth.

Sam: Interesting. I feel that different teachers come in our lives and give us lessons according to our needs.

SIRSHREE: Every lesson is useful at a given time. The student who constantly strides forward attains the final truth. Some students are not able to take the right decision; they get stuck or go astray. Some children indulge in fighting, playing, eating, drinking and making merry, and thereby miss out on the most precious time of their lives. They are not able to connect to the lessons being taught in their classes after the break. They are not able to concentrate on what is going on in the class. On the other hand, those children who spend their recess time in meeting people, making conversation, seeking advice and discussing issues, seize the opportunity of life with both hands. They can fully comprehend what is being taught in their classes after the break. They begin to enjoy their studies. They are not afraid of examinations.

Sam: Going back a little to what you added, what happens in these classes after the break, the recess?

Sirshree: There is a new teacher in the class when the pupils return to their classes after the break. The new teacher informs them, 'If you had any questions during the recess, I shall explain them to you. There is a principal of this school, who controls and administers the entire school. And there is life beyond this school. I shall explain to you with an example about what else happens in this school'.

The teacher continues, 'The example that I am going to tell you, has some very important indications or pointers, which you have to understand through contemplation. A class has five students. They studied throughout the year. Examinations were conducted at the end of the year. Some pupils passed the examinations, while others failed. Some students who failed are allowed to go to the higher class despite their failure. They will have to clear the subjects they failed in during the next class.

Let us suppose that the first and the second student passed the examination. The third student failed in some subjects and was given a provisional promotion. The fourth student failed because he did not study carefully. The fifth one did not appear for the examination as he had decided to drop out. All the students had to go to the examination board's office to get their results. When they went there, according to the rules of the office, they were shown their answer papers. The student who had decided to drop out also went along. But, of course, there was no paper of his. Everyone was going through their own papers. Those who had passed were seeing how they had done a good job but made some mistakes too. They were learning from their mistakes and thinking about how not to repeat them the next time. Those who had failed were trying to understand their major errors.

Those students who had passed were told that they would go to a higher class. For example, if they were in class five, they would go to class six. However, those who desired could also go to class seven. They were given an option to make a decision for themselves. One of the students who had passed said, 'I will go to class seven directly from class five'. He was warned that the syllabus of class seven was very difficult. He was also shown the syllabus. He, nevertheless, accepted the challenge. The other student who had passed said, 'I will go to class six as I will not be able to cope with studies in class seven at this stage'. Both the students made their decisions according to their abilities and understanding'. The teacher's example is not yet over. There is more. However, here is a question for you Sameer. If you were in their place, what decision would you have taken?

Sam: I would have jumped to class seven.

SIRSHREE: Then, look at problems in your life like that. It is your order. You wanted to take on a higher syllabus.

Sam: Yes, Sirshree.

SIRSHREE: The student who was given promotion despite failing in one subject was asked, 'If you go to class six, you will have to work really hard. Are you prepared for it?' He thought about it and replied, 'I am ready'. He had learnt from his past mistakes. He was now committed to start studying right from the beginning of the year in the new class.

The student who had failed was told that he would have to stay in the same class. He had no other choice. The student who had decided to drop out and had not given the examination, which is akin to taking one's own life, was told that he would have to go a step back. He would have to go to the previous class.

Does hearing this surprise you? In the school of life, some students are sent back to lower classes.

Sam: No, Sirshree. It is clear. In fact, I just loved your addition.

SIRSHREE: You have come on Earth to receive precisely this training. When you meet a true guru or spiritual master, you accept the truth first intellectually and then get trained experientially. He teaches you sadhana – the practice. Having gained the spiritual knowledge and the sadhana, when you want to react adversely to a situation or respond egoistically, you refrain from doing so and follow the teachings.

Sam: Wonderful explanation, Sirshree. The importance of your teachings are even more clear now. Reverting to the topic of life after death, I have one question, Sirshree. I understand that fear of death has been created so that people do not take their lives. But is there something else to fear? Is it true that unsatisfied subtle bodies turn into ghosts? Do they haunt us?

SIRSHREE: The world of subtle bodies is unknown because of which, we fear it unnecessarily. Just as we are able to survive and live comfortably in this world with wicked people all around us, likewise, we do not have to fear the other world. We live our lives with caution and awareness, and, thereby, feel quite comfortable. There are criminals in both the worlds. Do you live in constant fear of the criminals in this world?

Sam: No.

Sɪʀsʜʀᴇᴇ: However, you get scared when you hear about the criminals – ghosts and spirits – of the other world. Mischievous people are present in both the worlds. Do not be disturbed by this.

There are thieves in almost every city, town and village. You are aware that there may be thieves in or around your neighbourhood too. There is a possibility that in the middle of the night they can come and burgle your house. But do you start living in fear? Do you remain awake the entire night? No, you sleep soundly night after night. You just take the precaution of securing your house properly. You double lock the door to deter the thieves, you deploy the best security systems, and then you go off to sleep soundly.

Similarly, to avoid the mischievous elements of the other world, you just have to keep your thoughts positive. If you are not full of fears, if you do not have a feeble mind, then such things can never come close to you or harm you. You should have a positive attitude in both the worlds. You are not afraid when you read in newspapers about criminals in this world, then why should you get terrified on hearing even a story about ghosts and spirits from the other world? There is nothing to fear. Your contrast mind is the biggest ghost. It keeps on producing horrifying thoughts and suspicions, thereby scaring you like a ghost. But if your thoughts are positive, no harm can come to you from them.

Every person has a field of vibrations around him. This field is either positive or negative. What we repel or attract towards us depends on the kind of field that we create around us. The mischievous elements of the subtle world can trouble only those people who are of weak disposition, who think negatively and who have no thinking of their own. Such people get carried away by whatever thought comes into their minds at a particular point of time. They are easily influenced by others. If someone pushes them on the wrong path, they easily take that too. Those who have no direction or thinking are most vulnerable to such elements.

Sam: That means there are mischievous elements in the subtle world.

SIRSHREE: There are, but you will have no problem due to them. We develop a fear as a result of listening to ghost stories or seeing ghosts shown in movies. This is because the movie makers show everything in exaggeration to sell their movies. This happens on Earth as people of different levels of understanding live together. This does not happen in Part Two, as people there live on different subplanes according to their level of understanding and consciousness. Only those who have a higher level of consciousness will be living at the higher sub-planes. Those with lower level of consciousness will be living at lower sub-planes.

Sam: So, do ghosts exist?

SIRSHREE: There are no such ghosts as you imagine them to be. Movies, stories and folklore have painted a certain picture of ghosts and spirits, which is not true. The biggest ghost is seated within you. That ghost is your contrast mind. The contrast mind is being trained so that it becomes calm and silent, develops devotion, and gets detached from the past and the future. The contrast mind is conditioned to think about yesterday or tomorrow. It has to be trained to live in the present.

Negative energies, that we call ghosts and spirits, are attracted towards only those people who are receptive to such negative things. Such kinds of people are often negative thinkers or fearful people. Fearful people shrink within themselves and create space inside them for negative elements. Fearless and joyful people open up or expand. They do not have space left within them for negative energies.

Scared minds are porous like a sponge. A sponge absorbs any liquid poured on it because of its minute pores. Do not make your mind a sponge that will absorb negative vibrations. Whenever you feel scared, repeat the following mantra, 'I am God's child, no evil can touch me'. This mantra will close all your pores and help you overcome all your fears.

Sam: Thanks a lot for clearing this dubious subject! Actually, I had never been scared of ghosts, but I was always undecided about it. However, some people are very scared of ghosts.

SIRSHREE: A lot of people are fearful about astrology, the planets, ghosts, and so on. People think, 'My stars are not good. Why is this happening with me?' The answer to this question is that stars can affect only 10-15 per cent of your lives, not more than that. More than 90 per cent of the effect is due to your thoughts. External forces affect you only to the extent you allow them to affect you and if you are receptive to them. If most of your thoughts are negative, then even minor external forces will have a huge negative impact on your life.

If you have positive thoughts, the 10-15 per cent of planetary influence will not be able to affect you adversely. On the contrary, it will help you to progress and open new possibilities of happiness. Therefore, don't be afraid thinking that somebody is doing black magic on you; your planetary positions are not favourable or the astrologer told you that you will be facing difficulties for ten more years. Throw out all such things from your head and adopt a more positive outlook towards life to get the best out of life.

Sam: So, not only for fear of death or for fear of ghosts, what you say is applicable everywhere.

SIRSHREE: Yes. You encounter a number of problems and adverse situations in your life. Their purpose is to teach you how to become a better and stronger person. Whenever you are feeling low because of a problem, ask yourself, 'Is this problem going to kill me? Will I die due to this setback?' You will know the answer intuitively. It will be an emphatic 'No'. If the answer is 'Yes', then there is nothing left to ask. Thus what cannot slay you can only make you stronger. It is said, 'The way out of a difficulty is through it'. Face the challenges head on and emerge a much stronger person. You have to do a lot of great things ahead in life.

Learn to believe in the power of truth that is building up inside you. When you remember God while doing all your activities, the power of truth starts building up within you. Till now, you have collected a lot of negative energy – the energy of untruth within you. You are fortunate that it cannot match the power of the positive energy generated from the truth. Otherwise, you would have been dead by now. Untruth has the power only to create an illusion around you.

Untruth has only that much power which can create the 'I' or ego – the feeling of apparent separateness inside you. This is all that untruth can do – and it has done that. Untruth does not have much power, but truth has immense power. As many number of times you think about God throughout the day, in the same proportion the divine energy awakens within you. Nothing can bother you then.

While discharging all your duties on this Earth, even if all your problems have been solved, you will still be in trouble if you fail to attain self-realisation or the final truth. If you attain the final truth, you will be in bliss despite the presence of adversities. Therefore, we should resolve to keep an eye on the truth even while dealing with the many problems in life.

Sam: Wonderful, Sirshree! Thank you for letting us know the ultimate purpose of human life and for imparting the final truth to us through discourses and retreats.

Sɪʀsʜʀᴇᴇ: Our next meeting will be our last on this topic, Sameer. Having heard all this, the time has come for you to tell how you are modifying your life now for a better Part Two.

Sam: Yes, Sirshree. I can't wait till next Wednesday.

Sɪʀsʜʀᴇᴇ: And Sirshree shall reveal how you can reach the Supreme level of Consciousness. Thank you for the opportunity of serving you.

WEEK TEN

The Highest Creation

Sameer had already made a number of positive changes in his life. He and Mona together decided what kind of life they would like to lead so that they could train their minds.

Sameer discussed with Mona regarding what habits of his were harmful for his progress in Part One. He realised that they were harmful for his journey in Part Two also. Sameer, being an IT professional, created a tracker using a spread-sheet software for his life. He also created a document called 'No-no's in my life' and listed things that he wished to cut off from his life.

As Wednesday approached, he felt a little gloomy since this was his last encounter with Sirshree on the topic of death. The reason to meet the stabilised soul was over. Sameer wanted to pour his heart out and share everything about his experiences, his insights and his immense gratitude. But he knew he hadn't enough time in the meeting slot with Sirshree. This made him feel grateful as well as a little sad as he prepared to meet Sirshree on Wednesday.

Sam: I feel elated on knowing everything about death.
         I feel unhappy that this will be our last meeting.

SIRSHREE: You mean, the last meeting on this topic.

Sam: Yes. That's what I meant.

SIRSHREE: You said you felt elated that you know everything. But, Sirshree has revealed only 10 per cent.

Sam: What? Oh! How can I know the rest, Sirshree?

SIRSHREE: You need not know the rest now. Many things will become apparent as you get some insights. For understanding some things, your senses need to become sharper. And many things will become clear when you shed the gross body.

Sam: Amazing! And here I was thinking I knew everything. This thing about insights you were talking about, some things have already begun happening to me.

SIRSHREE: Such as?

Sam: I had an insight about confidence. I was taking a flight over the weekend. And despite being a frequent flyer, I always feel frightened during landings. As the plane was landing this time, I again felt frightened. That is when a thought struck me, 'What if the plane crashes and I die?' But then I realised there is nothing like death. I need not worry. And that was it. My fear evaporated. I am confident that it shall never come back again. And then I was thinking that if I no longer have the fear of death, that would make me one of the most confident individuals on Earth.

SIRSHREE: Everyone has the fear of death. And they do not realise that it is possible to have the understanding that shall liberate them from this fear – the understanding you have now.

Sam: And the best part of the understanding is that it does not make you reckless. It does not make you say, 'What the hell! I don't care if I die today'. In fact, I value life on Earth much more. One instance is that I drive more safely now.

SIRSHREE: Good...

Sam: Sorry for the interruption, Sirshree. Another thing has started to happen. That there is life after death has become intuitively obvious to me. So, it is no longer at an intellectual level. I can't explain what I mean by intuitive knowledge. All I can say is that it is a deeper feeling of understanding and acceptance with what you say. And then it struck me – you had said something else would happen when this knowledge sinks in. This was five weeks back when I had expressed my doubts. You had explained the five foundations on which these teachings are based. After hearing them, I had said that these foundations were beginning to make sense to me. At that time, you had mentioned something else would happen as things started making sense. Is this intuitive knowledge that I have now is what you were referring to then?

SIRSHREE: Yes, Sameer. Conviction arises. Like the conviction you have now.

Sameer: How do I know whether this conviction is correct or incorrect?

SIRSHREE: Conviction is conviction. You just know. However, if you do want a litmus test, then it is the state of your mind. Any conviction arising in an elevated state of mind is the truth.

Sameer: This is a great test. Another interesting thing happens. My logical mind still interferes and questions that maybe what I claim as my intuitive knowledge may actually be nothing but my faith in you. But then, I use logic to silence my logical mind.

SIRSHREE: How?

Sam: I say to myself that though there is enough logic and evidence, let us assume that all that Sirshree is saying is all humbug and untrue. Let's assume that it is all over at the end of this life. Then too, the changes I am making to my life now – believing that there is life after death would mean that I will live a better life now. And even if there is nothing at the end, I would have still lived a fulfilled life. Thus, a life lived believing there is life after death is much better than a life lived believing there is no life after death.

SIRSHREE: True, Sameer. And another thing that adds to the conviction is the experience of samadhi.

Sam: Yes, Sirshree. The existential experience felt in the retreat and the daily practice of sitting in samadhi that you have taught us does add to the conviction that my real nature is timeless and spaceless.

The feeling of consciousness, the experience of existence is undeniable.

SIRSHREE: When you are in samadhi, then the fifth, the Self, is being accessed. The Self experiences Itself.

Sam: Yes, Sirshree. Though the fear of death is not there, I do have a question. What will happen if I die at this moment? I mean, knowing me and my level of spiritual growth, what does Sirshree think will happen to me? Where do you think I will find a place in Part Two? Will it be on a higher plane?

SIRSHREE: Your question is like the one asked to Lord Mahavira in a famous story.

One day when Lord Mahavira was meditating, someone came and informed Him that a certain kingdom was going to be attacked by an army. They further told Him, 'The king of this kingdom which is going to be attacked has relinquished the throne some time back and is presently meditating in a jungle. Given that he has renounced his kingdom, he would certainly go to heaven and attain enlightenment'.

People of those times believed that the king who gave up his throne and kingdom attained enlightenment. This is because Lord Mahavira had renounced his kingdom and worldly possessions and so had Lord Buddha. People, therefore, thought that sons from rich or noble families who renounced their worldly possessions attained enlightenment.

That king in question had also given up his throne. His kingdom was going to be attacked. People asked Lord Mahavira, 'If the king dies at this moment, where will he go – to heaven or hell?' Lord Mahavira replied, 'He will go to hell'.

This puzzled those people as they wondered how someone, who was meditating and praying, could go to hell. After some time, they asked Him, 'Why do you say that he will go to hell?' Lord Mahavira closed his eyes and said, 'If he dies right now, he will go to heaven'.

When asked earlier, Lord Mahavira had replied that he will go to hell. Now, He was saying that he would attain heaven. Why did He say so? A person requested the Lord to clarify this point. Lord Mahavira explained, 'What was the state of mind of the king when you first asked me the question? He was meditating; but when he saw the army passing through the jungle and came to know that it was going to attack his kingdom, he got angry. He was filled with rage and hatred. If he had died at that moment, what would he have created? He would have created a hell for himself and that is where he would have gone'.

When Lord Mahavira later said that he would go to heaven, he said, 'After some time, understanding awakened in the king's mind. He realised that he was thinking his kingdom was going to be attacked. He had given up his kingdom, yet he still had the feeling of 'my kingdom'. This implied that he had not actually renounced it; he was still attached to his world. After this realisation dawned upon him, *viveka* – his power of discrimination and wisdom – awakened, and he let go of his attachment to 'I' and 'my'. If he died at that moment, he would die liberated. He would create heaven'.

Of course, Sameer, heaven or hell are not places that exist where people are sent after their physical death. In fact, everyone creates his own hell or heaven, and there are infinite possibilities for that. Humans can create anything they want. What is created by the enlightened Self is the highest form of expression because it arises from the highest level of understanding.

Sam: Does it mean that whatever thought I have at 'this moment' makes a difference if I were to die at this very moment?

SIRSHREE: No, no! Stories are narrated to inspire people and also to help people understand intricate knowledge easily. This story illustrates beautifully that your level of understanding and consciousness is what creates heaven or hell for you in the other world. If one thinks about the truth or God at the time of death, he will create a heaven. The missing link here is that those who have negative tendencies cannot create heaven. Only those who have attained understanding and thought about the truth all their lives will be able to think the same at the time of their death. Otherwise, they will not be able to remember the truth at the time of their death.

People have wrongly taken this as a shortcut to enlightenment. They believe that despite the good or bad that they do all their lives, if they take the name of God at the time of their death, they will achieve enlightenment. They believe that even if they christen their loved ones by the names of God and call them at their deathbed, God will come to them. Such blind shortcuts and easy ways have been handed down through false stories. Those who have made up such stories, as well as their followers, are both in the pits.

There are also the other types of so-called godmen who say, 'Everyone is the same after death regardless of whether he was a saint or a criminal during his Earthly life; therefore eat, drink and make merry'. They have not really understood what the enlightened saints have said. But the mind likes to follow such immoral advice. They go on to advise people saying, 'Supposing you were a saint or a criminal in your dreams, but after waking up you have become one and the same. Therefore, it does not really matter if you have done any wrongs in your life'. Such are the arguments given by them and the followers they attract are also those who want to indulge in wrong activities.

Sam: Thanks for clarifying, Sirshree. So, what do you think shall happen to me if I die at this very moment?

Sirshree: First, understand that if you die at this moment, the understanding you have about life here, about life after death and about accessing the Self shall be intact. Your mental sheath is carried forward...

Sam: And I shall live amidst those similar to the purity and clarity of my mental sheath. Based on what you know and read of me, what exactly will happen to me?

SIRSHREE: One thing is for sure. If you die today, then you shall not be able to enter the Supreme plane of Consciousness. You will be denied the opportunity of 'immaculate enlightenment invention'.

Sam: Oh, oh! I can't even repeat what you said... enlightenment invention?

SIRSHREE: At the highest level of consciousness – or one can say at the Supreme plane of Consciousness – immaculate enlightenment invention takes place. Sirshree calls it MNN.

Sam: Why MNN?

SIRSHREE: It is the second letter of these three very important words iMmaculate eNlightenment iNvention. Leave out the vowels at the beginning of each word, and you are left with MNN. In Hindi, it is *Maha Nirvan Nirman*.

Sam: Very beautiful choice of words indeed. You have always had a way with words, Sirshree. But what is this MNN? Immaculate means pure or perfect. So what is this perfect enlightenment invention?

SIRSHREE: You can call it as 'perfect enlightenment creation'. Immaculate enlightenment invention or MNN is what you create at the seventh level. There are so many things that have been created on this Earth. What are some of the best creations or inventions you can think of?

Sam: Well, the Taj Mahal is a great creation. The Internet is a fabulous invention.

SIRSHREE: What about music? What about yoga? What about mantras? What about prayer? What about meditation? What about dance? What about the Bible or Koran or Gita? Do you consider these as great creations as well or not?

Sam: Definitely. Music and dance, yoga, prayer, meditation, the Bible or Koran or Gita are definitely great creations. One may say they are greater creations than the Taj or the Internet.

SIRSHREE: Who created these? And why?

Sam: Well, the Taj was created by Emperor Shah Jahan in memory of his beloved wife. And the Internet was set up as ARPANET first by the US Department of Defense for better communication between their network of computers and those of academic institutions.

SIRSHREE: Sirshree was referring to the rest of the list. Who created various art forms?

Sam: I don't know who created music or dance. I know that Patanjali compiled the Yoga Sutras.

SIRSHREE: All of these – yoga, dance, music, prayer, devotional songs, sculpture, etc. were created by the enlightened. The first portrait or idol of God was created by the enlightened. They did it as an expression of Self. They did it to explain and make others experience God.

Sam: I believe that. Let us take Sufi songs. So many of these songs have been converted into movie songs today and people just love them.

SIRSHREE: What is created by the enlightened touches your heart and lingers for hundreds of years. Needless to say that the Gita or Koran or Bible or other holy books were also the creations of the enlightened.

   Jesus created a lot of things on Earth. Saint Dnyaneshwar took samadhi saying that the role of his gross body had ended. He did not need it further to create anything more on Earth. When they will go to the next world, what picture will they create? You just cannot imagine it. Even if you can imagine that picture, or supposing that picture is shown to you, you will say that the picture is not attractive and there is nothing remarkable about it. When those who have not attained enlightenment see pictures painted by the enlightened, they will say, 'What is so great about this picture? It has nothing'. They will then be told that this nothing is not the usual nothing. This nothing is everything [*God is nothingness*]. You need to have vision and understanding to interpret those pictures.

Similarly, analogies or words to explain God created by Ramana Maharshi or Ramakrishna Paramahamsa or Saint Dnyaneshwar are beautiful creations.

Sam: Or what you are doing. Your words are equally poignant.

SIRSHREE: And these creations were done on Earth, where there are limitations – limitations of the gross body, limitations of time, space, etc. At the Supreme level of Consciousness in Part Two, where there are no limitations, imagine what one can create! That is why it is called Immaculate Enlightened Invention or MNN.

Everyone is being trained in this life on Earth so that they can remain steadfast on the path of truth and get rid of their vices, addictions and tendencies. This is because whatever you will create after death would be based on the tendencies you have developed during your life on Earth. If you are free from all tendencies, you will create MNN.

After creating MNN – the supreme expression of the Self – you will realise that had you been stuck with your tendencies, what a blunder it would have been! This is because when tendencies and mental patterns dominate you, you want to satisfy your lower desires, and not create MNN.

Sam: How do our lower desires affect our creation in Part Two?

SIRSHREE: Let us understand this through some examples.

When a person goes from one room to another, people say that he has died, as he can no longer be seen by them. This is metaphorical. Now what is he creating in the other room? He had come in this room – the Earth – to collect some colours so that he could paint the canvas lying in the other room in Part Two. If you have not got trained in this room and die with hatred, what will you go and create in the other room? What dreadful pictures are you going to paint? But those who are trained and ready, what supreme creation will they come up with?

When someone who is visually impaired in Part One dies, he would want to satisfy his unfulfilled desires in the next world. He would want to watch the movies that he had not been able to see on Earth due to his blindness. They then try to gratify their unfulfilled desires even after death.

You may not be visually impaired. But, you may be steeped in ignorance. What will someone who is impaired by his negative patterns create? He will only try to satisfy the craving that has always been in his mind as all the disorders and deformities of the gross body cease to exist in the subtle body. The blind does not remain blind, the lame does not remain lame, and the deaf does not remain deaf. All the difficulties and diseases of the gross body end. But the shortcomings of the mind remain as they are; these do not go away because the same mind is still present with the subtle body. The old tendencies that are present in the mind remain the same. The understanding that you acquire on Earth also remains the same.

If a person does not attain wisdom, what will he create in the other world? If he has not acquired *Tejgyan* or final wisdom and hence lived his life believing himself to be the body, he will create only those things which satisfy his personal cravings and ego.

In the other world, as soon as he gets the opportunity, he will try to create whatever he has not been able to acquire on Earth. If at that point someone tries to tell him, 'Do not run after these things. You do not know what immense possibilities you have within you. You don't know what you are creating. You can create a great possibility. Stop creating things for your personal satisfaction; accept what you are doing right now', he will not agree. You will not be able to convince him as he does not possess the wisdom.

As is the habit, so is the creation. As are the desires, so are the actions. If there is a person who is crippled here, there he will create a field where he can run. He has never been able to run on Earth, so he would like to create a running track for himself. He will try to satisfy his desire which he had not been able to fulfil on Earth as he has harboured that desire within him for a long time. But we do not have to think about creating such things in the other world.

Just try to imagine the desires of a person who is perpetually hungry. If he gets enough money and power, what is he most likely to create? He will no doubt create a restaurant and food. What would be the desire of a person who is fearful? What would be the desire of a disabled person?

Sam: Oh! Is that so? That's very important information indeed! We seriously need to work on our desires and tendencies. But won't someone reach Part Two and gradually progress to MNN?

SIRSHREE: Sirshree wants you to enter MNN directly, not progress gradually. There is a risk that you may get stuck at one place. Only those who have learnt to completely discipline their minds, bodies and intellects on this Earth and those who have truly carried out spiritual practice will be able to create something great. Only they will be able to create MNN. Only they will be able to achieve supreme expression. The rest will waste all their time in satisfying their personal desires in Part Two, because when man is controlled by his tendencies, patterns and vices, he is not able to see the right path. He goes astray. Even while practising on Earth, we see how tendencies raise their ugly heads. Those tendencies tell us, 'Leave all this prayer and meditation for a while, you can practise it later'.

Meanwhile, the undisciplined mind craves for some comfort, some security, some gain, or some taste of food and drink. In this way, as old habits resurface, man is completely distracted and stops his practice and training midway. He abandons his pursuit of knowledge. He may even leave the path of truth. If we are not able to carry out spiritual practice with our gross bodies, how will we do so with our subtle bodies? If we are not able to walk straight on the road, how will we walk on a rope?

The more clearly we understand life after death and MNN, the better we will be able to understand the value of our time on this Earth. We will realise that no time can be wasted further. If we continue to live a life of carelessness and addictions, what will we create there?

Those who have attained supreme knowledge and wisdom will create MNN. When you tell them that they do not have to build a running track or a restaurant, they will understand easily. You will not face any problem with them. They are absolutely clear in their minds that they do not have to get into all such worthless pursuits. They will then immediately find themselves at a new level, and thus will be able to explore new possibilities. Those who have not acquired the Supreme Knowledge can only create hell with never-ending desires and miseries for themselves.

People of both kinds exist on Earth, even in the same home, as the Earth is a learning ground. It is a school to learn about life. You have to practise here in order to express yourself adequately in the other world. Those who will build hell here will continue to live in hell. Those who will create heaven will always live in heaven. But those who will create MNN will make the choice of supreme expression of the Self.

If you are aware about your purpose on this Earth, you will continue practising on the right track wherever you are, at home, at work or anywhere, and you will enjoy your practice. If you lose sight of your supreme goal, you will not be able to practice. You will not be able to learn the lessons of Supreme Life. You will be engrossed with petty worries and insecurities such as why did people not appreciate me? Why did they not clap for me? They appreciated me yesterday, so what happened today? That person was good with me yesterday, but why has he changed his attitude today?

To come out of such pettiness, you have to remember your sole purpose on Earth, and at the right time. It is critical to always remember your ultimate aim on Earth, lest you fritter away precious time. If our life just passes by without anyone telling us all these vital aspects about the truth, without us contemplating over our purpose of life and achieving it, it will be a complete waste. It is, therefore, necessary to understand what we are doing and why we are doing it. Who are we? We are learning and getting prepared in the school of Earth for the supreme and complete life ahead. So, now that you have understood what MNN is, tell Sirshree how you are preparing. How are you preparing for life after death in this life?

Sam: I have made a number of changes in my life. We have converted our home into a home ashram. We have decided to wake up at 7 am daily, made dietary changes, set up a system so that we don't miss a single silent meditation session and steadfastly practise the sadhana that Sirshree has imparted to us. Now there is a deep sense of urgency, especially on hearing about MNN. My original questions, with which I came to Sirshree ten sessions ago, are no longer there. The purpose of life is very clear to me now.

SIRSHREE: Good, Sameer. Sirshree wants you to live a complete life. That is the last lesson for today. That is the last message.

Sam: What is a 'complete life?'

SIRSHREE: 'Complete life' does not mean the lifespan of the gross body till its death. Death of the gross body is akin to reaching a halting place on a long journey, or a particular stage of life. The first stage consists of childhood until one reaches adolescence. The second stage is when one attains youth and the third is old age. When one leaves the gross body and continues on the journey of the subtle body through the process we call 'after death', that is the fourth stage.

Complete life means the life in which we have to attain understanding about supreme expression, supreme desire, and supreme choice. If you have understood this very clearly and your commitment is firm, you will not waste a single moment from now on. But if you are not aware, then it might take days, months or even years to awaken to the truth. You waste productive time sleeping. The practice that you had to undertake, the art of life that you had to learn on Earth, is not learnt.

Sam: Yes, Sirshree, Supreme Expression is clear, that is MNN. Supreme Desire is clear, that is attaining the Self. What is Supreme Choice?

SIRSHREE: Choosing the higher always. Making every decision considering the Highest – considering Part Two.

Sam: That's great! This is a great practice – to constantly ask myself what is the supreme choice possible.

SIRSHREE: Choice – keeping the complete picture in mind.

Sam: Yes, Sirshree. Thanks a ton for all these sessions. Any key message that you would like me to remember?

SIRSHREE: Yes, Sameer. The understanding that you acquire on this Earth is considered to be of utmost importance. The karma of understanding what you do here during your life as a human in Part One, is going to guide your life in the next world or Part Two. Therefore, all saints have emphasised on your karma or deeds.

Sam: What is karma, Sirshree?

SIRSHREE: For that we need some more sessions, Sameer. For now, understand that only one thing counts in Part Two, and that is your level of consciousness – your spiritual knowledge and understanding. And all deeds that lead you to that are important.

Sam: Great, Sirshree! This I shall remember. And I hope that I shall be able to meet you for ten more sessions on karma.

SIRSHREE: We will see. Thank you for the opportunity of serving you.

50 Key Points mentioned in the Book

1. When the unmanifest is manifested, the world is created. The manifested associates with a body and becomes an individual. The ego (the feeling of apparent separateness) within an individual produces fear of death. Knowledge of death makes us fearless.

2. In the human body on this Earth, there is unprecedented preparation going on. The person who is aware that there is life after death will not waste even a single moment of his life. He will learn his lessons from each incident, which will help him in enhancing his patience and prepare him for his future journey.

3. In the school of Earth, spend recess time in meeting people, talking to them, seeking information, opinions and advice, and in discussing matters together. This way, you can seize the opportunity of life and learn what you have come to learn.

4. Don't get scared of the difficulties in life and commit suicide. This will make your journey ahead in Part Two even more difficult.

5. The principal of the school of life is one and the same for everyone. He is known by different names such as Ishwar, God, Lord, Allah, Self, etc.

6. Ignorance about death is what makes it a monster. If we acquire the right knowledge about death, it will help us learn the art of life.

7. A person who knows the secret of life and has attained self-realisation will always be ready at the right time for the death of his body.

8. There is a single entity on this Earth that is vibrating at different frequencies and getting transformed into different forms. The final aim of man, the ultimate goal of each and every one of us, is to understand that entity. Our body is also vibrating and changing every single moment. It is dying every moment and being born every moment. That is why there is no need to fear death.

9. Every human being has four sheaths – the Physical sheath, the Pranic sheath, the Mental sheath and the Causal sheath. The fifth is the one Self operating those four sheaths. Your aim is to reach that fifth.

10. The effect of the aura present around a person is what is known as the personality. Those who have a strong personality have a big and strong aura around them. The aura shrinks in scared and timid people.

11. If a person is wearing a vest, a shirt, a sweater and a coat, that means he is separate from all these garments.

After so-called death, the two outer sheaths – the Physical and the Pranic – of a person are shed off; just like removing the coat and sweater. The shirt, the vest and the person wearing them continue with their journey.

12. When a person dies, it is just like shedding the car body. He now drives a scooter because the scooter and the person driving it are still alive. His journey continues with his subtle body (the scooter).

13. It seems like a man has died when he sheds off his gross body, but his journey continues with the subtle body. Our power of sight is limited therefore, when we cannot see the subtle body, we think that he has died.

14. Man experiences 'so-called death' when his gross body is shed off. This is because his journey continues with his subtle body after this death. Man actually dies when his subtle body dies.

15. When you are in deep sleep, many a time, your subtle body goes out and travels in the astral plane. This is the reason why people feel a sense of déjà-vu – that they have already seen a place even though they have never been to that place before.

16. Many people who are physically or mentally sick become absolutely fine just before their physical death. This is because they realise from their own experience that it is not real death. They understand this at the time of their death. You are, however, being given this supreme knowledge much before, which is very significant.

17. The thoughts that you harbour your entire life make an appearance even during your death. Therefore, if you have acquired complete wisdom through a guru during your life, you will have thoughts of the truth at the time of your death.

18. You recall your entire physical life during the grey period, which is the transition period between so-called death and the beginning of the journey of the subtle body. You are reminded to see the complete picture of your life before deciding whether your life was successful or not. Do not jump to conclusions midway.

19. The scale of time is different in the life of the subtle body as compared to the gross body. That is why it cannot be explained in our language about how long the subtle body will live, but it can be said that it will be a much longer life as compared to life on Earth.

20. If a person who has left his gross body has a desire to meet his relatives in the subtle world who have died before him, he can do so because the time scales are different in the subtle world as compared to the physical world.

21. Science is trying to find out about timelessness and spacelessness. It is predicted that within a certain period of time, people will know about newer dimensions. Scientific language will help in understanding the facts about life after death.

22. Pray for the person after his so-called death so that he may be able to commence on his journey ahead immediately. Prayers have a lot of power. The journey

ahead is more important for the subtle body. Pray for it and do not waste time crying.

23. Thoughts play the most important role in the subtle body. Therefore, always think positive and happy thoughts.

24. Your knowledge and understanding is your passport in the subtle world. Attain understanding while on this Earth and get rid of your false notions and beliefs.

25. In the journey of the subtle body, the more beliefs it sheds, the clearer it can see. Otherwise it will be embroiled in a long period of confusion.

26. Learn all your lessons while being in the gross body. Do not run away from the difficulties of life. It is *you* who has to learn your lessons; nobody else can do it for you. For example, your sister should not do your homework for you. Help others learn their lessons too.

27. The subtle body cannot be harmed by a stick or a stone; however, it can be harmed by words. For this reason, never criticise a person after his death; just pray for him.

28. Only those who have committed suicide face a lot of difficulties in the subtle body. Learn to face all your lessons on Earth. Learning just half of these lessons will result in a lot of difficulty in your journey ahead.

29. Rites and rituals performed after death have an underlying reason. If you are performing them with full understanding, then it is fine. They are futile if done out of fear or superstition. For this reason, always have understanding while performing rituals.

30. People fear subtle bodies thinking that they come back as ghosts and trouble them. There are no such ghosts as shown in movies. The biggest ghost is seated within you, and that ghost is your contrast mind.

31. The body and mind of people who are negative thinkers are receptive to negative energies termed ghosts and spirits. Negative elements can create mischief only in such bodies. Therefore, always keep positive thoughts and do not fear.

32. Heaven and hell do not appear after death. You carry your own heaven or hell with you in this world as well as the next, according to the thoughts you have. People have been given the fear of hell and greed of heaven so that they live a virtuous life on Earth.

33. He who is in hell does not realise that he is in hell. One who is in heaven knows that he is in heaven and that the other person is in hell. The one who is at a higher level can recognise lower levels. However, those who are at lower levels can never recognise higher levels.

34. Only 'Consciousness' or 'Self' that is within all of you has rebirths. A body can never have a rebirth. People have the misconception that the body undergoes rebirth. But it is not so. With the death of the gross body, the five elements of the body – ether, air, fire, water, and earth – get dissolved in the five elements of the Earth.

35. You have been born on this Earth in order to undergo training and practice so that you can create MNN in your subtle body. Therefore, it is imperative to learn

all your lessons completely on Earth.

36.   When one is involved in objects pertaining to his senses (taste, smell, touch, words or form), one is functioning through the gross body. When one harbours an imagination or desire, one is working through the mental sheath. When one is engrossed in deep contemplation or deep meditation, one is expressing himself through the causal sheath.

37.   The subtle world is made up of subtle or fine vibrations of light and colours and is hundreds of times bigger than the gross world (the Earth).

38.   People on Earth derive vital energy from air in order to sustain. People in the subtle world derive their energy from the Divine Light.

39.   If a person has lived a greedy, selfish and sinful life on Earth, he finds himself in a hazy, dark, gloomy, miserable and heavy atmosphere in the other world, which is ruled by fear and suffering.

40.   If the person who has died has been violent, greedy and self-centred on Earth, he will be surrounded by similar people in the other world. There is an atmosphere of darkness and hopelessness around him.

41.   If a person's life on Earth has been that of selfless service and empathy for others, the other world presents him with a life full of love, joy and beauty.

42.   As man progresses in the subtle world and brings purity in his thoughts, he adds radiance and beauty to his persona. That is why it is said that even while living on Earth, we should bring purity in our thoughts.

43. Those who are filled with love, compassion, selfless service and patience on this Earth reach the higher sub-planes after their so-called death depending on the degree of purity of their mind.

44. Encountering the truth in the other world, people wonder if they are the ones who are dead, or it is the people on Earth who are living under such a big illusion.

45. On this Earth we have three dimensions – length, breadth and height. In the other world, other than these three, there is a fourth dimension, which has never been expressed in our language.

46. No one can be cheated or misunderstood in that world. People act mostly on the basis of their intuition.

47. All activities in the subtle world take place with the help of thoughts, because it is thoughts that are the main power in that world. This is why you are told to always have positive thinking and happy thoughts.

48. Internal beauty is considered to be a spiritual quality in the subtle world, not the external appearance. That is why the subtle beings do not give much importance to the face.

49. Just as images produced by light can be seen to be moving about on the cinema screen, in the same way the subtle bodies, whose source of energy is light, are seen to be functioning in a systematic manner in the subtle world. They don't need oxygen for energy. People on Earth are able to sustain themselves due to the vital energy present in the solid, liquid and

gaseous forms, and in air. People in the subtle world live on light energy.

50.   The limited human consciousness finally gets liberated and chooses its role. It either guides people on Earth, or becomes instrumental for guiding the beings of the subtle world, or merges into the unlimited oneness or God.

For information on Sirshree, visit:
www.tejgyan.org

For more information on the
Magic of Awakening (MA) Retreat or for
any questions or feedback about this book,
please write to ma@tejgyan.com or
call +91 9011020854

For further details, contact:
Yogi Impressions Books Pvt. Ltd.
1711, Centre 1, World Trade Centre,
Cuffe Parade, Mumbai 400 005, India.

Fill in the Mailing List form on our website
and receive, via email, information on
books, authors, events and more.
Visit: www.yogiimpressions.com

Telephone: (022) 61541500, 61541541
Fax: (022) 61541542
E-mail: yogi@yogiimpressions.com

 Join us on Facebook:
www.facebook.com/yogiimpressions

 Follow us on Twitter:
www.twitter.com/yogiimpressions

ALSO PUBLISHED BY YOGI IMPRESSIONS

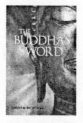

DVDs

AUDIO CDs

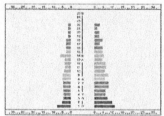 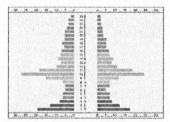